THE MIND LIKE FIRE UNBOUND

The Mind like Fire Unbound

An Image in the Early Buddhist Discourses

Ṭhānissaro Bhikkhu

(Geoffrey DeGraff)

Printed for free distribution

Very well then, my friend, I will give you an analogy; for there are cases where it is through the use of an analogy that intelligent people can understand the meaning of what is being said.

Contents

Abbreviations

References to DN, Iti, Khp, & MN are to discourse *(sutta)*. The reference to Mv is to chapter, section, & sub-section. References to other Pali texts are to section *(saṁyutta, nipāta,* or *vagga)* & discourse.

All translations are the author's own. Those from the Pali Canon are from the Royal Thai Edition (Bangkok: Mahamakut Rajavidyalaya, 1982).

Terms marked in the text with an asterisk (*) are explained in the End Notes.

Because Pali has many ways of expressing the word 'and,' I have—to avoid monotony—used the ampersand (&) to join lists of words & short phrases, and the word 'and' to join long phrases & clauses.

Preface

TO STUDY ANCIENT TEXTS is like visiting a foreign city: Time & inclination determine whether you want a quick, pre-packaged tour of the highlights, a less structured opportunity for personal exploration, or both. This book on the connotations of the words *nibbāna (nirvāṇa)* & *upādāna* in the early Buddhist texts is organized on the assumption that both approaches to the topic have their merits, and so it consists of two separate but related parts. Part I, The Abstract, is the quick tour—a brief survey to highlight the main points of the argument. Part II, The Essay, is a chance to make friends with the natives, soak up the local atmosphere, and gain your own insights. It takes a more oblique approach to the argument, letting the texts themselves point the way with a minimum of interference, so that you may explore & ponder them at leisure. Part I is for those who need their bearings and who might get impatient with the seeming indirection of Part II; Part II is for those who are interested in contemplating the nuances, the tangential connections, & the sense of context that usually get lost in a more structured approach.

Either part may be read on its own, but I would like to recommend that anyone seriously interested in the Buddha's teachings take the time to read reflectively the translations that form the main body of Part II. People in the West, even committed Buddhists, are often remarkably ignorant of the Buddha's original teachings as presented in the early texts. Much of what they know has been filtered for them, at second or third hand, without their realizing what was added or lost in the filtration. Although the quotations in Part II, by their sheer length & numbers, may at times seem like overkill, they are important for the context they give to the teachings. Once the teachings have context, you can have a surer sense of what is true Buddha Dhamma and what are filtration products.

This book has been many years in preparation. It began from a casual remark made one evening by my meditation teacher—

Phra Ajaan Fuang Jotiko—to the effect that the mind released is like fire that has gone out: The fire is not annihilated, he said, but is still there, diffused in the air; it simply no longer latches on to any fuel. This remark gave me food for thought for a long time afterwards. When I came to learn Pali, my first interest was to explore the early texts to learn what views they contained about the workings of fire and how these influenced the meaning of nibbāna—literally, 'extinguishing'—as a name for the Buddhist goal. The result of my research is this book.

Many people have helped in this project, directly or indirectly, and I would like to acknowledge my debts to them. First of all, Phra Ajaan Fuang Jotiko, in addition to being the original inspiration for the research, provided me with the training that has formed the basis for many of the insights presented here. The example of his life & teachings was what originally convinced me of Buddhism's worth. A. K. Warder's excellent *Introduction to Pali* made learning Pali a joy. Marcia Colish & J. D. Lewis, two of my professors at Oberlin College, taught me—with no small amount of patience— how to read & interpret ancient texts. Ven. Bhikkhu Bodhi, Donald Swearer, John Bullitt, Margaret Dornish, Robert Ebert, Michael Grossi, Lawrence Howard, & Doris Weir all read earlier incarnations of the manuscript and made valuable suggestions for improvements. I, of course, am responsible for any mistakes that may still remain.

Finally, I would like to dedicate this book in gratitude to my father, Henry Lewis DeGraff, and to the memory of my mother, Esther Penny Boutcher DeGraff, who taught me the value of truth, inner beauty, & goodness from an early age.

Ṭhānissaro Bhikkhu

(Geoffrey DeGraff)

Metta Forest Monastery
August, 1993

Part One:
The Abstract

ABSTRACT

"Released...with unrestricted awareness."

ACCORDING TO THE PALI CANON—the earliest extant record of the Buddha's teachings—the fabrications of language cannot properly be used to describe anything outside of the realm of fabrication. In one mode of analysis, this realm is divided into the six senses (counting the mind as the sixth) & their objects; in another mode, into the five aggregates of form, feeling, perception, fabrications, & consciousness. However, passages in the Canon (such as AN 4:173 and SN 35:117) point to another realm—where the six senses & their objects cease—which can be experienced although not otherwise described, even in terms of existing, not existing, both, or neither. The goal of Buddhist practice belongs to this second realm, and this of course raised problems for the Buddha in how to teach & describe that goal.

He solved the problem by illustrating the goal with similes & metaphors. The best-known metaphor for the goal is the name *nibbāna (nirvāṇa)*, which means the extinguishing of a fire. Attempts to work out the implications of this metaphor have all too often taken it out of context. Some writers, drawing on modern, everyday notions of fire, come to the conclusion that nibbāna implies extinction, inasmuch as we feel that a fire goes out of existence when extinguished. Others, however, note that the Vedas—ancient Indian religious texts that predate Buddhism by many thousands of years—describe fire as immortal: Even when extinguished it simply goes into hiding, in a latent, diffused state, only to be reborn when a new fire is lit. These writers then assume that the Buddha accepted the Vedic theory in its entirety, and so maintain that nibbāna implies eternal existence.

The weakness of both these interpretations is that they do not take into account the way the Pali Canon describes (1) the workings of fire, (2) the limits beyond which no phenomenon may be described, and (3) the precise implications that the Buddha himself drew from his metaphor in light of (1) & (2). The purpose of this essay is to place this metaphor in its original context to show what it was and was not meant to imply.

Any discussion of the way the Buddha used the term nibbāna must begin with the distinction that there are two levels of nibbāna (or, to use the original terminology, two nibbāna properties). The first is the nibbāna experienced by a person who has attained the goal and is still alive. This is described metaphorically as the extinguishing of passion, aversion, & delusion. The second is the nibbāna after death. The simile for these two states is the distinction between a fire that has gone out but whose embers are still warm, and one so totally out that its embers are cold. The Buddha used the views of fire current in his day in somewhat different ways when discussing these two levels of nibbāna, and so we must consider them separately.

To understand the implications of nibbāna in the present life, it is necessary to know something of the way in which fire is described in the Pali Canon. There, fire is said to be caused by the excitation or agitation of the heat property. To continue burning, it must have sustenance *(upādāna)*. Its relationship to its sustenance is one of clinging, dependence, & entrapment. When it goes out, the heat property is no longer agitated, and the fire is said to be freed. Thus the metaphor of nibbāna in this case would have implications of calming together with release from dependencies, attachments, & bondage. This in turn suggests that of all the attempts to describe the etymology of the word nibbāna, the closest is the one Buddhaghosa proposed in *The Path of Purification:* Un- *(nir)* + binding *(vāna):* Unbinding.

To understand further what is meant by the unbinding of the mind, it is also important to know that the word upādāna—the sustenance for the fire—also means clinging, and that according to the Buddha the mind has four forms of clinging that keep it in bondage: clinging to sensuality, to views, to precepts & practices, and to doctrines of the self. In each case, the clinging is the passion & desire the mind feels for these things. To overcome this clinging, then, the mind must see not only the drawbacks of these four objects of clinging, but, more importantly, the drawbacks of the act of passion & desire itself.

The mind does this by following a threefold training: virtue, concentration, & discernment. Virtue provides the joy & freedom from remorse that are essential for concentration. Concentration provides an internal basis of pleasure, rapture, equanimity, & singleness of mind that are not dependent on sensual objects, so that discernment can have the strength & stability it needs to cut through the mind's clingings. Discernment functions by viewing these clingings as part of a causal chain: seeing their origin, their passing away, their allure, the drawbacks of their results, &, finally, emancipation from them.

Although the Canon reports cases where individuals cut through all four forms of clinging at the same time, the more common pattern is for discernment first to cut through sensual clinging by focusing on the inconstancy & stressfulness of all sensory objects and on the worthlessness of any passion or desire directed to them. Thus freed, the mind can turn its discernment inward in a similar way to cut through its clinging to the practice of concentration itself, as well as to views in general and notions of 'self' in particular. Once it no longer views experience in terms of self, the entire self/not-self dichotomy collapses.

The mind at this point attains Deathlessness, although there is no sense of 'I' in the attainment. There is simply the realization, 'There is this.' From this point onward the mind experiences mental & physical phenomena with a sense of being dissociated from them. One simile for this state is that of a hide removed from the carcass of a cow: Even if the hide is then placed back on the cow, one cannot say that it is attached as before, because the connective tissues that once held the hide to the carcass—in other words, passion & desire—have all been cut (by the knife of discernment). The person who has attained the goal—called a Tathāgata in some contexts, an arahant in others—thus lives out the remainder of his/her life in the world, but independent of it.

Death as experienced by a Tathāgata is described simply as, 'All this, no longer being relished, grows cold right here.' All attempts to describe the experience of nibbāna or the state of the Tathāgata after death—as existing, not existing, both, or neither—are refuted by the Buddha. To explain his point, he again makes use of the metaphor of the extinguished fire, although here he draws on the Vedic view of latent fire as modified by Buddhist notions of what does and does not lie within the realm of valid description.

To describe the state of the Tathāgata's mind, there has to be a way of knowing what his/her consciousness is dependent on. Here we must remember that, according to the texts, a meditator may develop intuitive powers through the practice of concentration enabling him/her to know the state of another person's mind, or the destination of that person after death. To do so, though, that person's consciousness must be dwelling on a particular object, for it is only through knowledge of the object that the state of the mind can be known. With ordinary people this is no problem, for ordinary consciousness is always dependent on one object or another, but with Tathāgatas this is impossible, for their consciousness is totally independent. Because terms such as existing, not existing, both, or neither, apply only to what may be measured against a criterion of knowing, they cannot apply to the Tathāgata.

The Buddha borrows two points from the Vedic notion of fire to illustrate this point. Even if one wants to assume that fire still exists after being extinguished, it is (1) so subtle that it cannot be perceived, and (2) so diffuse that it cannot be said to go to any one place or in any particular direction. Just as notions of going east, west, north, or south do not apply to an extinguished fire, notions of existing and so forth do not apply to the Tathāgata after death.

As for the question of how nibbāna is experienced after death, the Buddha says that there is no limit in that experience by which it could be described. The word 'limit' here is the important one. In one of the ancient Vedic myths of creation, the universe starts when a limit appears that separates male from female, sky from earth. Thus the implication of the Buddha's statement is that the experience of nibbāna is so free from even the most basic notions making up the universe that it lies beyond description. This implication is borne out by other passages stating that there is nothing in that experience of the known universe—earth, water, wind, fire, sun, moon, darkness, coming, going, or stasis—at all.

Thus, when viewed in light of the way the Pali Canon describes the workings of fire and uses fire imagery to describe the workings of the mind, it is clear that the word nibbāna is primarily meant to convey notions of freedom: freedom in the present life from agitation, dependency, & clinging; and freedom after death from even the most basic concepts or limitations—such as existence, non-existence, both, or neither—that make up the describable universe.

> Here, Hemaka,
> with regard to things that are dear
> —seen, heard, sensed, & cognized—
> there is: the dispelling of desire & passion,
> the undying state of Unbinding.
>
> Those knowing this, mindful,
> fully extinguished/unbound
> in the here & now,
> are forever calmed,
> have crossed over
> entanglement in the world.
>
> *Sn 5:8*

Freed, disjoined, & released from ten things, the Tathāgata dwells with unrestricted awareness, Vāhuna. Which ten? Freed, disjoined, & released from form…feeling…perception…fabrications…consciousness…birth…aging…death…stress*…defilement, he dwells with unrestricted awareness. Just as a red, blue, or white lotus born in the water and growing in the water, rises up above the water and stands with no water adhering to it, in the same way the Tathāgata—freed, disjoined, & released from these ten things—dwells with unrestricted awareness.

> *AN 10:81*

Just as the great ocean has but one taste, the taste of salt, even so does this doctrine & discipline have but one taste: the taste of release.

> *AN 8:19*

Part Two:
The Essay

"The enlightened go out like this flame."

THE DISCOURSES of the Pali Canon make a frequent analogy between the workings of fire and those of the mind: The mind unawakened to the supreme goal is like a burning fire; the awakened mind, like a fire gone out. The analogy is made both indirectly & directly: indirectly in the use of terminology borrowed from the physics of fire to describe mental events (the word *nibbāna* being the best-known example); directly in any number of metaphors:

> I have heard that on one occasion the Blessed One—while staying at Uruvelā on the bank of the Nerañjarā River in the shade of the Bodhi tree, newly awakened—was sitting in the shade of the Bodhi tree for seven days in one session, sensitive to the bliss of release. After the passing of those seven days, on emerging from that concentration, he surveyed the world with the eye of an Awakened One. As he did so, he saw living beings burning with the many fevers and aflame with the many fires born of passion, aversion, & delusion.
>
> *Ud 3:10*

> The All is aflame. Which All is aflame? The eye is aflame. Forms are aflame. Eye-consciousness is aflame. Eye-contact is aflame. And whatever there is that arises in dependence on eye'contact, experienced as pleasure, pain, or neither pleasure nor pain, that too is aflame. Aflame with what? Aflame with the fire of passion, the fire of aversion, the fire of delusion. Aflame, I tell you, with birth, aging, & death, with sorrows, lamentations, pains, distresses, & despairs.
>
> The ear is aflame. Sounds are aflame....
> The nose is aflame. Aromas are aflame....
> The tongue is aflame. Flavors are aflame....
> The body is aflame. Tactile sensations are aflame....

The intellect is aflame. Ideas are aflame. Intellect-consciousness is aflame. Intellect-contact is aflame. And whatever there is that arises in dependence on intellect-contact, experienced as pleasure, pain or neither pleasure nor pain, that too is aflame. Aflame with what? Aflame with the fire of passion, the fire of aversion, the fire of delusion. Aflame, I tell you, with birth, aging, & death, with sorrows, lamentations, pains, distresses, & despairs.

                                        SN 35:28

The fire of passion burns in a mortal
        excited, smitten, with sensuality;
the fire of aversion, in a malevolent person
        taking life;
the fire of delusion, in a bewildered person
        ignorant of the noble Dhamma.

Not understanding these fires, people
        —fond of self-identity—
unreleased from the shackles of death,
swell the ranks of hell,
        the wombs of common animals, demons,
        the realm of the hungry shades.

While those who, day & night,
        are devoted to the message
        of the One Rightly Self-awakened,
put out the fire of passion,
        constantly perceiving the repulsive.
They, superlative people, put out the fire of aversion
                with good will,
and the fire of delusion
        with the discernment leading to penetration.

They, masterful, untiring by night & day,
        having put out [the fires],
having, without remainder,
understood stress,
go, without remainder,
        totally out.

They, the wise, with an attainer-of-wisdom's
      noble vision
   with regard to right gnosis,
directly knowing the ending of birth,
   return to no further becoming.*

Iti 93

   Not only is the extinguishing of passion, aversion, & delusion
compared to the extinguishing of a fire, but so is the passing away
of a person in whom they are extinguished.

Ended the old,
      there is no new taking birth.
Dispassioned their minds
      toward future becoming,
they, with no seed,
      no desire for growth,
the enlightened go out
      like this flame.

Khp 6

Sister Sumedhā:

This, without aging,
      this without death,
this, the unaging, undying state
      with no sorrow,
         hostility,
         bonds,

   with no burning....

Thig 16:1

When the Blessed One was totally gone out—simultaneously
with the total going out—Ven. Anuruddha uttered these
stanzas:

He had no in-&-out breathing,
the one who was Such*, the firm-minded one.

imperturbable & bent on peace:
the sage completing his span.

With heart unbowed
he endured the pain.
Like a flame's going out
was the liberation
of awareness.

DN 16

The aim of this essay is to explore the implications of this imagery—to give a sense of what it was & was not intended to convey—by first making reference to the views concerning the physics of fire current in the Buddha's time. This, short of an actual experience of Awakening—something no book can provide—seems the most natural approach for drawing the proper inferences from this imagery. Otherwise, we are bound to interpret it in terms of our own views of how fire works, a mistake as misleading & anachronistic as that of painting a picture of the Buddha dressed as Albert Einstein or Isaac Newton.

The presentation here is more like a photomosaic than an exposition. Quotations have been aligned & overlapped so as to reflect & expand on one another. Comments have intentionally been kept to a bare minimum, so as to allow the quotations to speak for themselves. The weakness of this approach is that it covers several fronts at once and can make its points only incrementally. Its strength lies in its cumulative effect: revealing—beneath apparently disparate teachings—unifying patterns that might go unnoticed in a more linear narrative, much as satellite pictures can reveal buried archeological remains that would go unnoticed by a person standing on the ground.

One of the noteworthy features of the Pali Canon is that common patterns of thought & imagery shape the extemporaneous words of a wide variety of people reported within it. Here we will hear the voices not only of the Buddha—the speaker in all passages from the Canon where none is identified—but also of lay people such as Citta, monks such as Vens. Ānanda & MahāKaccāyana, and nuns such as Sisters Nandā, Sumedhā, & Pāṭācārā. Each has his or her own style of expression, both in poetry & in prose, but they all speak from a similarity of background & experience that makes it possible to view their message as a single whole, in structure as well as content.

The structure we are most concerned with here centers on the image of extinguished fire and its implications for the word *'nibbāna' (nirvāṇa)* & related concepts. Used with reference to fire, nibbāna means 'being out' or 'going out.' Used with reference to the mind, it refers to the final goal and to the goal's attainment. Our essay into the cluster of meanings surrounding this word is meant to read like a journey of exploration, but a brief preview will help us keep track both of where we are in relation to the map provided by the Abstract, and of where we are going.

The first chapter surveys ancient Vedic ideas of fire as subsisting in a diffused state even when extinguished. It then shows how the Buddha took an original approach to those ideas to illustrate the concept of nibbāna after death as referring not to eternal existence, but rather to absolute freedom from all constraints of time, space, & being.

The remaining three chapters deal with the concept of nibbāna in the present life. Chapter II introduces a cluster of Buddhist ideas concerning the nature of burning fire—as agitated, clinging, bound, & dependent—and draws out the implications that these ideas have for what happens when a fire goes out and, in parallel fashion, when the mind attains nibbāna. In particular, it concludes that of all the etymologies traditionally offered for nibbāna, Buddhaghosa's 'unbinding' is probably closest to the original connotations of the term.

Chapter III takes up the notion of clinging as it applies to the mind—as sensuality, views, habits & practices, and doctrines of the self—to show in detail *what* is loosened in the mind's unbinding, whereas Chapter IV shows *how*, by detailing the way in which the practice of virtue, concentration, & discernment frees the mind from its fetters. This final chapter culminates in an array of passages from the texts that recapitulate the pattern of fire-&-freedom imagery covered in the preceding discussion. If read reflectively, they also serve as reminders that their perspectives on the concept of nibbāna can best be connected only in light of that pattern.

We should note at the outset, though, that nibbāna is only one of the Buddhist goal's many names. One section of the Canon lists 33, and the composite impression they convey is worth bearing in mind:

> The unfashioned, the end,
> the effluent-less*, the true, the beyond,
> the subtle, the very-hard-to-see,
> the ageless, permanence, the undecaying,
> the surface-less, non-objectification,
> peace, the deathless,
> the exquisite, bliss, solace,
> the exhaustion of craving,
> the wonderful, the marvelous,
> the secure, security,
> nibbāna,
> the unafflicted, the passionless, the pure,
> release, non-attachment,
> the island, shelter, harbor, refuge,
>
> the ultimate.

SN 42:1-44

CHAPTER I

"This fire that has gone out...
in which direction from here has it gone?"

THE DISCOURSES report two instances where brāhmans asked the Buddha about the nature of the goal he taught, and he responded with the analogy of the extinguished fire. There is every reason to believe that, in choosing this analogy, he was referring to a concept of fire familiar to his listeners, and, as they had been educated in the Vedic tradition, that he probably had the Vedic concept of fire in mind. This, of course, is not to say that he himself adhered to the Vedic concept or that he was referring to it in all its details. He was simply drawing on a particular aspect of fire as seen in the Vedas so that his listeners could have a familiar reference point for making sense of what he was saying.

Now, although the Vedic texts contain several different theories concerning the physics of fire, there is at least one basic point on which they agree: Fire, even when not manifest, continues to exist in a latent form. The Vedic view of all physical phenomena is that they are the manifestation of pre-existent potencies inherent in nature. Each type of phenomenon has its corresponding potency, which has both personal & impersonal characteristics: as a god and as the powers he wields. In the case of fire, both the god & the phenomenon are called Agni:

> Agni, who is generated, being produced [churned] by men through the agency of *sahas*.
>
> > *RV 6,48,5*

'*Sahas*' here is the potency, the power of subjugation, wielded by Agni himself. Jan Gonda, in discussing this passage, comments, 'The underlying theory must have been...that a man and his physical strength are by no means able to produce a god or potency of Agni's rank. Only the co-operation or conjunction of that special principle which seems to have been central in the descriptions of

Agni's character, his power of subjugation, his overwhelming
power, can lead to the result desired, the appearance of sparks
and the generation of fire.' Further, 'a divine being like Agni was
in a way already pre-existent when being generated by a pair of
kindling sticks' (1957, pp. 22-3). As fire burns, Agni 'continues
entering' into the fire (AV 4,39,9). Scattered in many places—as
many separate fires—he is nevertheless one & the same thing (RV
3,55). Other fires are attached to him as branches to a tree (RV 8,19).

When fire is extinguished, Agni and his powers do not pass out
of existence. Instead, they go into hiding. This point is expressed
in a myth, mentioned frequently in the Vedic texts, of Agni's try-
ing to hide himself from the other gods in places where he thought
they would never perceive him. In the version told in RV 10,51,
the gods finally find the hidden Agni as an embryo in the water.

> [Addressed to Agni]: Great was the membrane & firm, that
> enveloped you when you entered the waters....We searched
> for you in various places, O Agni, knower of creatures,
> when you had entered into the waters & plants.
>
> *RV 10,51*

As Chauncey Blair notes, 'The concept of Agni in the waters
does not imply destruction of Agni. He is merely a hidden, a
potential Agni, and no less capable of powerful action' (1961, p. 103).

The implications of Agni's being an embryo are best understood
in light of the theories of biological generation held in ancient
India:

> The husband, after having entered his wife, becomes an
> embryo and is born again of her.
>
> *Laws of Mānu, 9,8*

Just as ancient Indians saw an underlying identity connecting
a father & his offspring, so too did they perceive a single identity
underlying the manifest & embryonic forms of fire. In this way,
Agni, repeatedly reborn, was seen as immortal; and in fact, the

Vedas attribute immortality to him more frequently than to any other of the gods.

> To you, immortal! When you spring to life, all the gods sing for joy....By your powers they were made immortal....[Agni], who extended himself over all the worlds, is the protector of immortality.
>
> *RV 6,7*

Not only immortal, but also omnipresent: Agni in his manifest form is present in all three levels of the cosmos—heaven, air, & earth—as sun, lightning, & flame-fire. As for his latent presence, he states in the myth of his hiding, 'my bodies entered various places'; a survey of the Vedas reveals a wide variety of places where his embryos may be found. Some of them—such as stone, wood, plants, & kindling sticks—relate directly to the means by which fire is kindled & fueled. Others relate more to fire-like qualities & powers, such as brilliance & vitality, present in water, plants, animals, & all beings. In the final analysis, Agni fills the entire universe as the latent embryo of growth & vitality. As Raimundo Panikkar writes, 'Agni...is one of the most comprehensive symbols of the reality that is all-encompassing' (1977, p.325).

> Agni pervades & decks the heaven & earth...his forms are scattered everywhere.
>
> *RV 10,80*

> He [Agni] who is the embryo of waters, embryo of woods, embryo of all things that move & do not move.
>
> *RV 1,70,2*

> In plants & herbs, in all existent beings, I [Agni] have deposited the embryo of increase. I have engendered all progeny on earth, and sons in women hereafter.
>
> *RV 10,183,3*

You [Agni] have filled earth, heaven, & the air between, and
follow the whole cosmos like a shadow.

RV 1,73,8

We call upon the sage with holy verses, Agni Vaiśvānara the
ever-beaming, who has surpassed both heaven & earth in
greatness. He is a god below, a god above us.

RV 10,88,14.

This view that Agni/fire in a latent state is immortal & omnipresent occurs also in the Upaniṣads that were composed circa
850-750 B.C. and later accepted into the Vedic Canon. The authors
of these texts use this view to illustrate, by way of analogy, the
doctrines of a unitary identity immanent in all things, and of the
immortality of the soul in spite of apparent death.

Now, the light that shines higher than this heaven, on the
backs of all, on the backs of everything, in the highest
worlds, than which there are no higher—truly that is the
same as the light here within a person. There is this hearing
of it—when one closes one's ears and hears a sound, a roar,
as of a fire blazing.

ChU 3.13.7-8

Truly, this Brahma [the god that the Upaniṣads say is
immanent in the cosmos] shines when fire blazes, and
disappears when it does not blaze. Its brilliance goes to
the sun; its vital breath to the wind.

This Brahma shines when the sun is seen, and disappears
when it is not seen. Its brilliance goes to the moon, its vital
breath to the wind. [Similarly for moon & lightning.]

Truly, all these divinities, having entered into wind, do not
perish when they die [disappear] in the wind; indeed, from
there they come forth again.

KauU 2.12

In the major non-canonical Upaniṣads—whose period of composition is believed to overlap with the time of the Buddha—the analogy is even more explicit:

> As the one fire has entered the world
> and becomes corresponding in form to every form,
>
> so the Inner Soul of all things
> corresponds in form to every form,
>   and yet is outside.
>
> *KaṭhU 2.2.9*

> As the material form of fire,
> when latent in its source,
>   is not perceived—
> and yet its subtle form
>   is not destroyed,
> but may be seized again
>   in its fuel-source—
>
> so truly both [the universal Brahmā
>   & the individual soul]
>   are [to be seized]in the body
>   by means of [the meditation word] AUM.
>
> Making one's body the lower friction stick,
>   and AUM the upper stick,
> practicing the drill of meditative absorption,
>   one may see the god,
>   hidden as it were.
>
> *ŚvU 1.13-14*

One interesting development in this stratum of the Vedic literature is the positive sense in which it comes to regard extinguished fire. The Vedic hymns & earlier Upaniṣads saw burning fire as a positive force, the essence of life & vitality. These texts, though, see the tranquility & inactivity of the extinguished fire as an ideal image for the soul's desired destination.

To that God, illumined by his own intellect,
do I, desiring liberation, resort for refuge—
    to him without parts,
      without activity,
        tranquil,
      impeccable, spotless,
the highest bridge to the deathless,
like a fire with fuel consumed.

                                ŚvU 6.18-19

As fire through loss of fuel
    grows still [extinguished] in its own source,
so thought by loss of activeness
    grows still in its own source....

For by tranquility of thought
 one destroys
    good & evil karma.
With tranquil soul, stayed on the Soul,
one enjoys
        unending ease.

                                MaiU 6.34

Whether this re-evaluation of the image of fire—seeing its extinguishing as preferable to its burning—predated the founding of Buddhism, was influenced by it, or simply paralleled it, no one can say for sure, as there are no firm dates for any of the Upaniṣads. At any rate, in both stages of the Vedic attitude toward fire, the thought of a fire going out carried no connotations of going out of existence at all. Instead, it implied a return to an omnipresent, immortal state. This has led some scholars to assume that, in using the image of an extinguished fire to illustrate the goal he taught, the Buddha was simply adopting the Vedic position wholesale and meant it to carry the same implications as the last quotation above: a pleasant eternal existence for a tranquil soul.

But when we look at how the Buddha actually used the image of extinguished fire in his teachings, we find that he approached the Vedic idea of latent fire from another angle entirely: If latent fire is everywhere all at once, it is nowhere in particular. If it is conceived as always present in everything, it has to be so loosely defined that it has no defining characteristics, nothing by which it might be known at all. Thus, instead of using the subsistence of latent fire as an image for immortality, he uses the diffuse, indeterminate nature of extinguished fire as understood by the Vedists to illustrate the absolute indescribability of the person who has reached the Buddhist goal.

> Just as the destination of a glowing fire
> struck with a [blacksmith's] iron hammer,
> gradually growing calm,
> isn't known:
>
> Even so, there's no destination to describe
> for those who are rightly released
> —having crossed over the flood
> of sensuality's bonds—
> for those who've attained
>
> unwavering ease.
>
> Ud 8:10

'But, Venerable Gotama [the brāhman, Aggivessana Vacchagotta, is addressing the Buddha], the monk whose mind is thus released: Where does he reappear?'

'"Reappear," Vaccha, doesn't apply.'

'In that case, Venerable Gotama, he does not reappear.'

'"Does not reappear," Vaccha, doesn't apply.'

'...both does & does not reappear.'

'...doesn't apply.'

'...neither does nor does not reappear.'

'...doesn't apply.'....

'At this point, Venerable Gotama, I am befuddled; at this point, confused. The modicum of clarity coming to me from your earlier conversation is now obscured.'

'Of course you're befuddled, Vaccha. Of course you're confused. Deep, Vaccha, is this phenomenon, hard to see, hard to realize, tranquil, refined, beyond the scope of conjecture, subtle, to-be-experienced by the wise. For those with other views, other practices, other satisfactions, other aims, other teachers, it is difficult to know. That being the case, I will now put some questions to you. Answer as you see fit. How do you construe this, Vaccha: If a fire were burning in front of you, would you know that, "This fire is burning in front of me"?'

'...yes...'

'And suppose someone were to ask you, Vaccha, "This fire burning in front of you, dependent on what is it burning?" Thus asked, how would you reply?'

'...I would reply, "This fire burning in front of me is burning dependent on grass & timber as its sustenance."'

'If the fire burning in front of you were to go out, would you know that "This fire burning in front of me has gone out"?'

'...yes...'

'And suppose someone were to ask you, "This fire that has gone out in front of you, in which direction from here has it gone? East? West? North? Or south?" Thus asked, how would you reply?'

'That doesn't apply, Venerable Gotama. Any fire burning dependent on a sustenance of grass & timber, being unnourished—from having consumed that sustenance and not being offered any other—is classified simply as "out" [*nibbuto*].'

'Even so, Vaccha, any form by which one describing the Tathāgata would describe him: That the Tathāgata has abandoned, its root destroyed, made like a palmyra stump, deprived of the conditions of existence, not destined for future arising. Freed from the classification of form, Vaccha, the Tathāgata is deep, boundless, hard-to-fathom, like the sea.

"Reappears" doesn't apply. "Does not reappear" doesn't apply. "Both does & does not reappear" doesn't apply. "Neither reappears nor does not reappear" doesn't apply.

'Any feeling...Any perception...Any fabrication...

'Any consciousness by which one describing the Tathāgata would describe him: That the Tathāgata has abandoned.... Freed from the classification of consciousness, Vaccha, the Tathāgata is deep, boundless, hard-to-fathom, like the sea.'

MN 72

The person who has attained the goal is thus indescribable because he/she has abandoned all things by which he/she could be described. This point is asserted in even more thoroughgoing fashion in a pair of dialogues where two inexperienced monks who have attempted to describe the state of the Tathāgata after death are cross-examined on the matter by Sāriputta & the Buddha himself.

Sāriputta: How do you construe this, my friend Yamaka: Do you regard form as the Tathāgata?

Yamaka: No, friend.

Sāriputta: Do you regard feeling as the Tathāgata?

Yamaka: No, friend.

Sāriputta: ...perception...?

Yamaka: No, friend.

Sāriputta: ...fabrications...?

Yamaka: No, friend.

Sāriputta: ...consciousness...?

Yamaka: No, friend.

Sāriputta: Do you regard the Tathāgata as being in form? Elsewhere than form? In feeling? Elsewhere than feeling? In perception? Elsewhere than perception? In fabrications? Elsewhere than fabrications? In consciousness? Elsewhere than consciousness?

Yamaka: No, friend.

Sāriputta: Do you regard the Tathāgata as form-feeling-perception-fabrications-consciousness?

Yamaka: No, friend.

Sāriputta: Do you regard the Tathāgata as that which is without form, without feeling, without perception, without fabrications, without consciousness?

Yamaka: No, friend.

Sāriputta: And so, my friend Yamaka—when you can't pin down the Tathāgata as a truth or reality even in the present life—is it proper for you to declare, 'As I understand the Teaching explained by the Blessed One, a monk with no more effluents, on the break-up of the body, is annihilated, perishes, & does not exist after death'?

Yamaka: Previously, friend Sāriputta, I did foolishly hold that evil supposition. But now, having heard your explanation of the Teaching, I have abandoned that evil supposition, and the Teaching has become clear.

Sāriputta: Then, friend Yamaka, how would you answer if you are thus asked: A monk, a worthy one, with no more effluents, what is he on the break-up of the body, after death?

Yamaka: Thus asked, I would answer, 'Form...feeling... perception... fabrications...consciousness are inconstant. That which is inconstant is stressful. That which is stressful has stopped and gone to its end.'

SN 22:85

The Buddha puts the same series of questions to the monk Anurādha who—knowing that the Tathāgata after death could not be described in terms of existence, non-existence, both, or neither—

had attempted to describe the Tathāgata in other terms. After receiving the same answers as Yamaka had given Sāriputta, the Buddha concludes:

> 'And so, Anurādha—when you can't pin down the Tathāgata as a truth or reality even in the present life—is it proper for you to declare, "Friend, the Tathāgata—the supreme man, the superlative man, attainer of the superlative attainment— being described, is described otherwise than with these four positions: The Tathāgata exists after death, does not exist after death, both does & does not exist after death, neither exists nor does not exist after death"?'
>
> 'No, lord.'
>
> 'Very good, Anurādha. Both formerly & now, Anurādha, it is only stress that I describe, and the stopping of stress.'
>
> *SN 22:86*

Thus none of the four alternatives—reappearing/existing, not reappearing/existing, both, & neither—can apply to the Tathāgata after death, because even in this lifetime there is no way of defining or identifying what the Tathāgata is.

To identify a person by the contents of his or her mind—such things as feelings, perceptions, or fabrications—there would have to be a way of knowing what those contents are. In ordinary cases, the texts say, this is possible through either of two cognitive skills that a meditator can develop through the practice of meditation and that beings on higher planes of existence can also share: the ability to know where a living being is reborn after death, and the ability to know another being's thoughts.

In both skills the knowledge is made possible by the fact that the ordinary mind exists in a state of dependency on its objects. When a being is reborn, its consciousness has to become estab- lished at a certain point: This point is what a master of the first skill perceives. When the ordinary mind thinks, it needs a mental object to act as a prop or support (*ārammaṇa*) for its thoughts: This support is what a master of the second skill perceives. The mind of a person who has attained the goal, though, is free from all dependencies and so offers no means by which a master of either skill can perceive it.

> Then the Blessed One went with a large number of monks to the Black Rock on the slope of Isigili. From afar he saw Ven. Vakkali lying dead on a couch. Now at that time a smokiness, a darkness was moving to the east, moving to the west, moving to the north, the south, above, below, moving to the intermediate directions. The Blessed One said, 'Monks, do you see that smokiness, that darkness...?'
>
> 'Yes, lord.'
>
> 'That is Māra*, the Evil One. He is searching for the consciousness of Vakkali the clansman: "Where is the consciousness of Vakkali the clansman established?" But, monks, through unestablished consciousness, Vakkali the clansman has attained total nibbāna.'
>
> *SN 22:87*

[The Buddha describes the meditative state of a person who has achieved the goal and is experiencing a foretaste of nibbāna after death while still alive. We will discuss the nature of this meditative state below. Here, though, we are interested in how this person appears to those who would normally be able to fathom another person's mind.]

There is the case, Sandha, where for an excellent thoroughbred of a man the perception of earth with regard to earth has ceased to exist; the perception of liquid with regard to liquid...the perception of heat with regard to heat...the perception of wind with regard to wind...the perception of the dimension of the infinitude of space with regard to the dimension of the infinitude of space...the perception of the dimension of the infinitude of consciousness with regard to the dimension of the infinitude of consciousness...the perception of the dimension of nothingness with regard to the dimension of nothingness...the perception of the dimension of neither perception nor non-perception with regard to the sphere of neither perception

nor non-perception...the perception of this world with
regard to this world...the next world with regard to the next
world...and whatever is seen, heard, sensed, cognized,
attained, sought after, pondered by the intellect: the
perception with regard even to that has ceased to exist.

Absorbed in this way, the excellent thoroughbred of a man
is absorbed dependent neither on earth, liquid, heat, wind,
the dimension of the infinitude of space, the dimension of
the infinitude of consciousness, the dimension of
nothingness, the dimension of neither perception nor non-
perception, this world, the next world; nor on whatever is
seen, heard, sensed, cognized, attained, sought after or
pondered by the intellect—and yet he is absorbed. And to
this excellent thoroughbred of a man, absorbed in this way,
the gods, together with Indra, the Brahmās & their viceroys,
pay homage even from afar:

> Homage to you, O thoroughbred man.
>   Homage to you, O superlative man—
> of whom we have no direct knowledge
>   even by means of that with which
>   you are absorbed.
>
> *AN 11:10*

Thus the mind that has attained the goal cannot be known or
described from the outside because it is completely free of any
dependency—any support or object inside it—by which it might
be known. This point forms the context for the dialogue in which
the brāhman Upasīva asks the Buddha about the person who
attains the goal.

> *Upasīva:*
>   If he stays there, O All-around Eye,
>   unaffected for many years,
>   right there
>   would he be cooled & released?
>   Would [his] consciousness become like that?

The Buddha:
> As a flame overthrown by the force of the wind
>   goes to an end not fitting to classify,
> so the sage freed from naming (mental) activity
>   goes to an end not fitting to classify.

Upasīva:
> He who has reached the end:
>   Does he not exist,
>   or is he for eternity free from affliction?
> Please, sage, declare this to me
>   as this phenomenon has been known by you.

The Buddha:
> One who has reached the end has no criterion
> by which anyone would say that—
>   for him it doesn't exist.
> When all phenomena are done away with,
> done away are all means of speaking as well.

Sn 5:6

The important term in the last verse is *pamāṇa:* 'criterion'. It is a pregnant term, with meanings both in philosophical and in ordinary usage. In philosophical discourse, it refers to a means of knowledge or a standard used to assess the validity of an assertion or object. In the Buddha's time and later, various schools of thought specialized in discussing the nature and role of such criteria. The Maitri Upaniṣad contains one of their basic tenets:

> Because of its precision, this [the course of the sun through the zodiac] is the criterion for time. *For without a criterion, there is no ascertaining the things to be assessed.*

MaiU 6.14

Thus when a mind has abandoned all phenomena, there is no means or criterion by which anyone else could know or say anything about it. This much is obvious. But the verse also seems to be saying that the goal is indescribable from the inside—for the person experiencing it—as well. First, the verse is in response to

Upasiva's inquiry into the goal *as the Buddha has known it.*
Secondly, the line, 'for him it doesn't exist,' can mean not only
that the person experiencing the goal offers no criteria to the
outside by which anyone else might describe him/her, but also
that the experience offers no criteria from the inside for describing
it either. And as we have already noted, the outside criteria by
which a person might be described are determined precisely by
what is there inside the person's mind. Thus, for the person
experiencing the goal, there would not even be any means of
knowing whether or not there was a person having the
experience. There would simply be the experience in & of itself.

This is where the ordinary meaning of pamāṇa—as limit or
measurement—comes in. This meaning goes back to the Vedic
hymns. There, the act of measuring is seen as an essential part of
the process of the creation (or 'building,' like a house) of the
cosmos. In one Ṛg Vedic hymn (X.129), for example, the creation
of mind is followed by the appearance of a horizontal limit or
measuring line separating male from female (heaven from earth).
From this line, the rest of the cosmos is laid out.

So to say that no criterion/measurement/limit exists for the
person experiencing the goal means that the person's experience
is totally free of all the most elementary perceptions & distinctions that underlie our knowledge of the cosmos. And the word
'free'—one of the few the Buddha uses in a straightforward way to
describe the mind that has attained the goal—thus carries two
meanings: free from dependency, as we have already seen; and
free from limitations, even of the most abstruse & subtlest sort.

This second reading of the verse—dealing with the limitless-
ness & indescribability of the goal for the person experiencing
it—is supported by a number of other passages in the Pali Canon
referring explicitly to the inner experience of the goal.

> Consciousness without surface, without end,
>   luminous all around:
> Here water, earth, fire, & wind have no footing.
> Here   long & short,
>   coarse & fine,

> fair & foul,
> name & form
> are all brought to an end.
> With the stopping
> of [sensory] consciousness,
>   each is here brought to an end.
>
>   *DN 11*

There is, monks, that dimension where there is neither earth
nor water, nor fire nor wind, nor dimension of the infinitude
of space, nor dimension of the infinitude of consciousness,
nor dimension of nothingness, nor dimension of neither
perception nor non-perception, nor this world, nor the next
world, nor sun, nor moon. And there, I say, there is neither
coming, nor going, nor stasis, nor passing away, nor arising:
without stance, without foundation, without support
[mental object]. This, just this, is the end of stress.

                              Ud 8:1

> Where water, earth, fire, & wind have no footing:
> There the stars do not shine,
>   the sun is not visible,
>   the moon does not appear,
>   darkness is not found.
>
> And when a brāhman, a sage through sagacity
>   has known [this] for himself,
> then from form & formless,
>   from pleasure & pain,
>
>   he is freed.
>
>   *Ud 1:10*

Consciousness without surface, without end, radiant all
around, is not experienced through the solidity of earth, the
liquidity of water, the radiance of fire, the windiness of
wind, the divinity of devas [and so on through a list of the
various levels of godhood to] the allness of the All.

                              MN 49

The phrase 'the allness of the All' can best be understood with reference to the following three passages:

> What is the All? Simply the eye & forms, ear & sounds, nose & aromas, tongue & flavors, body & tactile sensations, intellect & ideas. This, monks, is termed the All. Anyone who would say, 'Repudiating this All, I will describe another,' if questioned on what exactly might be the grounds for his statement, would be unable to explain, and furthermore, would be put to grief. Why? Because it lies beyond range.
>
> *SN 35:23*

If the six senses & their objects—sometimes called the six spheres of contact—constitute the All, is there anything beyond the All?

> MahāKoṭṭhita: With the remainderless stopping & fading of the six spheres of contact [vision, hearing, smell, taste, touch, & intellection] is it the case that there is anything else?
>
> Sāriputta: Don't say that, my friend.
>
> MahāKoṭṭhita: With the remainderless stopping & fading of the six spheres of contact, is it the case that there is not anything else?
>
> Sāriputta: Don't say that, my friend.
>
> MahāKoṭṭhita: ...is it the case that there both is & is not anything else?
>
> Sāriputta: Don't say that, my friend.
>
> MahāKoṭṭhita: ...is it the case that there neither is nor is not anything else?
>
> Sāriputta: Don't say that, my friend.
>
> MahāKoṭṭhita: Being asked...if there is anything else, you say, 'Don't say that, my friend'. Being asked...if there is not anything else...if there both is & is not anything else... if there neither is nor is not anything else, you say, 'Don't

say that, my friend'. Now, how is the meaning of this statement to be understood?

Sāriputta: Saying...is it the case that there is anything else... is it the case that there is not anything else...is it the case that there both is & is not anything else...is it the case the there neither is nor is not anything else, one is objectifying the non-objectified. However far the six spheres of contact go, that is how far objectification goes. However far objectification goes, that is how far the six spheres of contact go. With the remainderless fading & stopping of the six spheres of contact, there comes to be the stopping, the allaying of objectification.

AN 4:173

The dimension of objectification, although it may not be described, may be realized through direct experience.

Monks, that dimension should be experienced where the eye [vision] stops and the perception [label] of form fades. That dimension should be experienced where the ear stops and the perception of sound fades...where the nose stops and the perception of aroma fades...where the tongue stops and the perception of flavor fades...where the body stops and the perception of tactile sensation fades...where the intellect stops and the perception of idea/phenomenon fades: That dimension should be experienced.

SN 35:117

This experience of the goal—absolutely unlimited freedom, beyond classification and exclusive of all else—is termed the elemental nibbāna property with no 'fuel' remaining *(anupādisesa-nibbāna-dhātu)*. It is one of two ways in which nibbāna is experienced, the distinction between the two being expressed as follows:

Monks, there are these two forms of the nibbāna property. Which two? The nibbāna property with fuel remaining, and the nibbāna property with no fuel remaining.

And what is the nibbāna property with fuel remaining? There is the case where a monk is an arahant whose effluents have ended, who has attained completion, finished the task, laid down the burden, attained the true goal, destroyed the fetter of becoming, and is released through right gnosis. His five [sense] faculties still remain and, owing to their being intact, he experiences the pleasing & the displeasing, and is sensitive to pleasure & pain. His ending of passion, aversion, & delusion is termed the nibbāna property with fuel remaining.

And what is the nibbāna property with no fuel remaining? There is the case where a monk is an arahant...released through right gnosis. For him, all that is sensed, being unrelished, will grow cold right here. This is termed the nibbāna property with no fuel remaining.

Iti 44

The phrase referring to the range of feeling as 'growing cold right here' is a set expression describing death as experienced by one who has reached the goal. The verse following this passage states explicitly that this is what is meant here.

These two   proclaimed
          by the one with vision
nibbāna properties the one independent
          the one who is Such:

one property, here in this life
with fuel remaining
    from the ending of [craving],
    the guide to becoming

and that with no fuel remaining
    after this life
in which becomings
    entirely stop.

Those who know this unfabricated state,
their minds released
through the ending of [craving],
the guide to becoming,

they, attaining the Teaching's core,
delighting in ending,
have abandoned all becomings:
they, the Such.

Iti 44

The Verses of the Elder Udāyin suggest a simile to illustrate the distinction between these two nibbāna properties:

A great blazing fire
unnourished grows calm
and though its embers exist
is said to be out:
Conveying a meaning,
this image is taught by the cognizant.

Great Nāgas* will recognize
the Nāga as taught by the Nāga
as free from passion,
free from aversion,
free from delusion,
without effluent.

His body discarded, the Nāga
will go totally out
without effluent.

Thag 15:2

Here Ven. Udāyin compares the nibbāna property with fuel remaining—the state of being absolutely free from passion, aversion, & delusion—to a fire whose flames have died out, but whose embers are still glowing. Although he does not complete the analogy, he seems to imply that the nibbāna property without fuel remaining—when the Worthy One discards his body at death—is like a fire so totally out that its embers have grown cold.

Thus the completely free & unadulterated experience we have
been discussing is that of nibbāna after death. There are, though,
states of concentration which give a foretaste of this experience in
the present life and which enabled the Buddha to say that he taught
the goal on the basis of direct knowledge.

> Ānanda: In what way, venerable sir, might a monk attain
> concentration of such a form that he would have neither
> the perception of earth with regard to earth, nor of water
> with regard to water, nor of fire...wind...the dimension of
> the infinitude of space...the dimension of the infinitude
> of consciousness...the dimension of nothingness...the
> dimension of neither perception nor non-perception...
> this world...nor of the next world with regard to the next
> world, and yet he would still be percipient?

> The Buddha: There is the case, Ānanda, where he would be
> percipient of this: 'This is peace, this is exquisite— the
> resolution of all fabrications; the relinquishing of all
> acquisitions; the ending of craving; dispassion; stopping;
> nibbāna.'
>
> *AN 10:6*

[Ānanda puts the same question to Sāriputta, who responds
that he himself once had experienced such a concentration.]

> Ānanda: But what were you percipient of at that time?

> Sāriputta: 'The stopping of becoming—nibbāna—the
> stopping of becoming—nibbāna': One perception arose
> in me as another perception stopped. Just as in a blazing
> woodchip fire, one flame arises as another flame stops,
> even so, 'The stopping of becoming—nibbāna—the
> stopping of becoming—nibbāna': One perception arose
> in me as another one stopped. I was percipient at that
> time of 'the stopping of becoming—nibbāna.'
>
> *AN 10:7*

Ānanda: It is amazing, my friend, it is marvelous, how the
Blessed One has attained & recognized the opportunity
for the purification of beings...and the direct realization
of nibbāna, where the eye will be, and forms, and yet one
will not be sensitive to that dimension; where the ear will
be, and sounds...where the nose will be, and aromas...
where the tongue will be, and flavors...where the body
will be, and tactile sensations, and yet one will not be
sensitive to that dimension.

Udāyin: Is one insensitive to that dimension percipient or
not percipient?

Ānanda: ... percipient...

Udāyin: ... percipient of what?

Ānanda: There is the case where—with the complete
transcending of perceptions of form, and the passing
away of perceptions of resistance, and not attending to
perceptions of diversity—(perceiving,) 'infinite space,'
one remains in the dimension of the infinitude of space:
Percipient in this way, one is not sensitive to that
dimension.

Further, with the complete transcending of the
dimension of the infinitude of space, (perceiving,)
'infinite consciousness,' one remains in the dimension of
the infinitude of consciousness: Percipient in this way,
one is not sensitive to that dimension.

Further, with the complete transcending of the
dimension of the infinitude of consciousness, (perceiving,)
'There is nothing,' one remains in the dimension of
nothingness: Percipient in this way, one is not sensitive
to that dimension.

Once, friend, when I was staying in Sāketa at the Game
Refuge in the Black Forest, the nun Jaṭilā Bhāgikā went
to me and, on arrival—having bowed to me—stood to
one side. As she was standing to one side, she said to me:
'Ven. Ānanda, the concentration whereby—neither
pressed down nor forced back, nor with fabrications kept

blocked or suppressed—still as a result of release, contented as a result of stillness, and as a result of contentment one is not agitated: This concentration is said by the Blessed One to be the fruit of what?'

I said to her, '...This concentration is said by the Blessed One to be the fruit of gnosis [the knowledge of full Awakening].' Percipient in this way, friend, one is not sensitive to that dimension.

AN 9:37

In this extraordinary state of mental poise—neither pressed, forced, blocked, or suppressed—nibbāna in the present life is experienced as freedom from all perception dealing with the six sensory spheres & the dimensions of meditative absorption. Although one is conscious, and these dimensions are present, one does not partake of them.

On the level of ordinary sensory experience, however, nibbāna in the present life is experienced by the Worthy One as the passing away of passion, aversion, & delusion. This implies that these three states are analogous to fire; and as we saw in the Introduction, they are directly referred to as fires at various points in the Canon. On the surface, the notion of passion & aversion as fires hardly requires explanation, but in order to gain a fuller appreciation of the analogies that the Canon draws between fire on the one hand, and passion, aversion, & delusion on the other, we first need some background on the specifically Buddhist views on fire it contains.

CHAPTER II

"Fire burns with clinging,
and not without clinging."

ALTHOUGH THE COMPILERS of the Pali Canon were not
concerned with teaching the physical sciences, there are frequent
passages where they cite the behavior of the physical universe, in
similes or examples, to illustrate points of doctrine. A number of
these passages discuss questions of heat, motion, meteorology,
the etiology of diseases, and so forth, in enough detail to show
that a common theory underlies their explanation. That theory
centers on the concept of *'dhātu,'* property or potential. The
physical properties presented in this theory are four: those of earth
(solidity), liquid, heat, & wind (motion). Three of them—liquid,
heat, & wind—are potentially active. When they are aggravated,
agitated or provoked—the Pali term here, *'pakuppati'*, is used also
on the psychological level, where it means angered or upset—
they act as the underlying cause for activity in nature. Fire, for
example, is said to occur when the heat property is provoked.

> There comes a time when the external heat property is
> provoked and consumes village, town & city, countryside &
> rural area; and then, coming to the edge of a green district,
> the edge of a road, the edge of a rocky district, to the
> water's edge, or to a lush, well-watered area, goes out from
> lack of sustenance.
>
> *MN 28*

Once a fire has been provoked, it needs *'upādāna'*—commonly
translated as fuel—to continue burning. Upādāna has other
meanings besides fuel, though—one is the nourishment that
sustains the life & growth of a tree—and as we will see below,
wind can also function as a fire's upādāna. Thus, 'sustenance'
would seem to be a more precise translation for the term.

'How do you construe this, young man: Which fire would
be more brilliant, luminous, & dazzling—that which burned
in dependence on a sustenance of grass & timber, or that
which burned in dependence on having relinquished a
sustenance of grass & timber?'

'If it were possible, Gotama, for a fire to burn in dependence
on having relinquished a sustenance of grass & timber, that
fire would be the more brilliant, luminous, & dazzling.'

'It's impossible, young man, there is no way that a fire could
burn in dependence on having relinquished a sustenance of
grass & timber, aside from a feat of psychic power....'

MN 99

'Just as a fire, Vaccha, burns with sustenance, and not without
sustenance, even so I declare the rebirth of one who has
sustenance, and not of one without sustenance.'

'But, Venerable Gotama, at the moment a flame is being
swept on by the wind and goes a far distance, what do you
say is its sustenance then?'

'Vaccha, when a flame is being swept on by the wind and
goes a far distance, I say that it is wind-sustained. The
wind, Vaccha, is its sustenance at that time.'

'And at the moment when a being sets this body aside and
has not yet attained another body, what do you say is its
sustenance then?'

'Actually, Vaccha, when a being sets this body aside and has
not yet attained another body, I say that it is craving-
sustained. Craving, Vaccha, is its sustenance at that time.'

SN 44:9

Another meaning for upādāna is clinging, which suggests that,
just as a tree clings to the soil that provides its sustenance, fire
clings to its fuel. Thus the above passage could also read, 'fire
burns with clinging and not without clinging'—a characteristic of

fire that was observed in other ancient Asian traditions, such as
the Chinese I Ching, as well.

The clinging nature of fire is reflected in a number of other
idioms used by the Pali Canon to describe its workings. For one,
an object that catches fire is said to get 'stuck' (passive) or to 'stick'
(active): Adherence is a two-way process.

> Just as a wing bone or tendon parings, monks, thrown into
> a fire don't catch fire [lit: 'stick' or 'get stuck'], keep apart,
> turn aside, and are not drawn in; even so the heart of a
> monk who spends time often with a mind accustomed to
> focusing on the repulsive, doesn't stick to the [thought of]
> engaging in the sexual act, keeps apart, turns aside, and is
> not drawn in, and remains either indifferent or repelled.
>
> *AN 7:46*

The second side of the attachment—that fire, in sticking to
something, gets stuck—is reflected in yet another idiom in the
Pali Canon: When it leaves a piece of fuel it has been clinging to,
it is said to be released.

> Just as fire...after being released from a house of reeds or
> a house of grass, burns even gabled houses, plastered,
> latched, shut against the wind; even so, all dangers that
> arise, arise from fools, and not from wise people; all
> disasters...all troubles that arise, arise from fools and not
> from wise people.
>
> *MN 115*

This sense of fire's being entrapped as it burns echoes the
stanza from the Śvetāśvatara Upaniṣad, quoted above (page 19),
that refers to fire as being 'seized' when ignited by the friction of
fire sticks. Apparently the Buddhists were not alone in their time
in seeing attachment & entrapment as they watched a fire burn.
And this would account for the way early Buddhist poetry tends
to couple the image of an extinguished fire with the notion of
freedom:

like a flame's *going out*
was the *liberation* of awareness.

DN 16

as a *flame overthrown* by the force of the wind...
so the sage *freed* from naming activity...

Sn 5:6

So, to summarize: The image of an extinguished fire carried no connotations of annihilation for the early Buddhists. Rather, the aspects of fire that to them had significance for the mind-fire analogy are these: Fire, when burning, is in a state of agitation, dependence, attachment, & entrapment—both clinging & being stuck to its sustenance. Extinguished, it becomes calm, independent, indeterminate, & unattached: It lets go of its sustenance and is released.

This same nexus of events, applied to the workings of the mind, occurs repeatedly in Canonical passages describing the attainment of the goal:

One attached is unreleased; one unattached is released. Should consciousness, when standing [still], stand attached to form, supported by form [as its object], established on form, watered with delight, it would exhibit growth, increase, & proliferation. Should consciousness, when standing [still], stand attached to feeling...to perception... to fabrications...it would exhibit growth, increase, & proliferation. Were someone to say, 'I will describe a coming, a going, a passing away, an arising, a growth, an increase, or a proliferation of consciousness apart from form, from feeling, from perception, from fabrications,' that would be impossible.

If a monk abandons passion for the property of form... feeling...perception... fabrications...consciousness, then owing to the abandoning of passion, the support is cut off, and there is no base for consciousness. Consciousness, thus unestablished, not proliferating, not performing any function, is released. Owing to its release, it stands still. Owing to its stillness, it is contented. Owing to its contentment, it is not agitated. Not agitated, he [the monk] is totally 'nibbāna-ed' right within. He discerns that 'Birth is ended, the holy life fulfilled, the task done. There is nothing further for this world.'

SN 22:53

This being the set of events—stillness, independence, unattachment—associated with the extinguishing of a fire and the attainment of the goal, it would appear that of all the etymologies offered to explain the word 'nibbāna,' the one closest to its original connotations is that quoted by Buddhaghosa in *The Path of Purification* (VIII, 247). There he derives the word from the negative prefix '*nir*,' plus '*vāna*,' or binding*: 'Unbinding'.

Modern scholars have tended to scorn this derivation as fanciful, and they favor such hypotheses as 'blowing out,' 'not blowing' or 'covering.' But although these hypotheses may make sense in terms of modern Western ideas about fire, they are hardly relevant to the way nibbāna is used in the Canon. Freedom, on the other hand, is more than relevant. It is central, both in the context of ancient Indian theories of fire and in the psychological context of attaining the goal: 'Not agitated, he is totally unbound right within.'

So 'Unbinding' would seem to be the best equivalent for nibbāna we have in English. What kind of unbinding? We have already gained some idea—liberation from dependency & limitations, from agitation & death—but it turns out that nibbāna is not the only term the Buddha borrowed from the workings of fire to describe the workings of the mind. Upādāna is another, and a survey of how he applied it to the mind will help to show what is loosed in the mind's unbinding and how.

CHAPTER III

"Forty cartloads of timber."

UPĀDĀNA carries both of its meanings—clinging & sustenance—when applied to the mind. It refers on the one hand both to mental clinging & to the object clung to, and on the other to both the act of taking mental sustenance & the sustenance itself. This, of course, raises the question, 'Sustenance for what?' In the description of dependent co-arising, upādāna forms the condition for becoming and, through becoming, for birth, aging, death, and the entire mass of suffering & stress. Thus the answer: 'Sustenance for becoming' & its attendant ills.

> Just as if a great mass of fire, of ten...twenty...thirty or forty cartloads of timber were burning, and into it a man would periodically throw dried grass, dried cow dung, & dried timber, so that the great mass of fire—thus nourished, thus sustained—would burn for a long, long time; even so, monks, in one who keeps focusing on the allure of those phenomena that offer sustenance [lit: 'flammable phenomena'], craving develops; with craving as condition, sustenance; with sustenance as condition, becoming; with becoming as condition, birth; with birth as condition, aging, illness & death, sorrow, lamentation, pain, distress, & despair all come into play. Thus is the origin of this entire mass of suffering & stress.

> Just as if a great mass of fire...were burning, into which a man simply would *not* periodically throw dried grass, dried cow dung, or dried timber, so that the great mass of fire—its original sustenance being consumed, and no other being offered—would, without nourishment, go out; even so, monks, in one who keeps focusing on the drawbacks of those phenomena that offer sustenance, craving stops. From the stopping of craving, sustenance stops. From the stopping of sustenance, becoming...birth...aging, illness & death, sorrow, lamentation, pain, distress, & despair all stop. Thus is the stopping of this entire mass of suffering & stress.

> *SN 12:52*

The Buddha made a distinction between phenomena that offer sustenance & the sustenance itself.

> And what, monks, are phenomena that offer sustenance? What is sustenance? Form, monks, is a phenomenon offering sustenance. Any desire or passion related to it, is sustenance related to it. Feeling...Perception...Fabrications... Consciousness is a phenomenon offering sustenance. Any desire or passion related to it, is sustenance related to it.
>
> *SN 22:121*

Thus passion & desire are both the act of taking sustenance and the sustenance itself, while form, feeling, perception, fabrications, & consciousness simply offer the opportunity for them to occur.

Alternatively, we can translate the distinction as one between clingable phenomena & the clinging itself.

> And what, monks, are clingable phenomena? What is clinging? Form, monks, is a clingable phenomenon. Any desire or passion related to it, is clinging related to it. Feeling...Perception...Fabrications...Consciousness is a clingable phenomenon. Any desire or passion related to it, is clinging related to it.
>
> *SN 22.121*

In this case, passion & desire are the act of clinging and the object clung to, while form, feeling, & the rest simply offer the opportunity for them to occur.

Still, the two sides of this distinction are so closely interrelated that they are hardly distinct at all.

> Visākha: Is it the case that clinging/sustenance is the same thing as the five aggregates for clinging/sustenance [form, feeling, perception, fabrications, & consciousness], or is it something separate?

Sister Dhammadinnā: Neither is clinging/sustenance the same thing as the five aggregates for clinging/ sustenance, my friend, nor is it something separate. Whatever desire & passion there is with regard to the five aggregates for clinging/sustenance, that is the clinging/sustenance there.

MN 44

(The use of the word aggregate *(khandha)* here may relate to the fire image, as khandha can also mean the trunk of a tree.)

The desire & passion for these five aggregates can take any of four forms.

Monks, there are four [modes of] sustenance for becoming. Which four? Sensuality as a form of sustenance, views as a form of sustenance, habits & practices as a form of sustenance, doctrines of the self as a form of sustenance.

MN 11

These four modes of sustenance act as the focus for many of the passages in the Canon describing the attainment of the goal. Because they are so closely related to the notion of nibbāna—they are the binding loosened in the unbinding of the mind—each of them deserves to be considered in detail.

First, **sensuality.** The Buddha recommended relinquishing attachment to sensuality, not because sensual pleasures are in any way evil, but because the attachment itself is dangerous: both in terms of the pain experienced when a relished pleasure inevitably ends, and in terms of the detrimental influence such attachment can have on a person's actions—and thus on his or her future condition.

It is with a cause, monks, that sensual thinking occurs, and not without a cause....And how is it, monks, that sensual thinking occurs with a cause and not without a cause? In dependence on the property of sensuality there occurs the perception of sensuality. In dependence on the perception of sensuality there occurs the resolve for sensuality... the desire

for sensuality...the fever for sensuality...the quest for
sensuality. Questing for sensuality, monks, an uninstructed,
run-of-the-mill person conducts himself wrongly through
three means: through body, through speech, & through
mind....

Just as if a man were to throw a burning firebrand into a
dry, grassy wilderness and not quickly stamp it out with his
hands & feet, and thus whatever animals inhabiting the
grass & timber would come to ruin & loss; even so, monks,
any contemplative or brāhman who does not quickly
abandon, dispel, demolish, & wipe out of existence an out-
of-tune, unskillful perception once it has arisen, will dwell
in stress in the present life—threatened, despairing, &
feverish—and on the break-up of the body, after death, can
expect a bad destination.

                                             SN 14:12

This is not to deny that sensual pleasures provide a certain
form of happiness, but this happiness must be weighed against
the greater pains & disappointments sensuality can bring.

Now what is the allure of sensuality? There are, monks,
these five strings of sensuality. Which five? Forms cognizable via the eye—agreeable, pleasing, charming, endearing,
fostering desire, enticing. Sounds cognizable via the ear...
Aromas cognizable via the nose...Flavors cognizable via the
tongue...Tactile sensations cognizable via the body—agreeable, pleasing, charming, endearing, fostering desire, enticing.
Now whatever pleasure or joy arises in dependence on these
five strings of sensuality, that is the allure of sensuality.

And what is the drawback of sensuality? There is the case
where, on account of the occupation by which a clansman
makes a living—whether checking or accounting or calcu-
lating or plowing or trading or cattle tending or archery or as
a king's man, or whatever the occupation may be—he faces
cold, he faces heat, being harassed by mosquitoes & flies,
wind & sun & creeping things, dying from hunger & thirst.

Now this drawback in the case of sensuality, this mass of stress visible here & now, has sensuality for its reason, sensuality for its source, sensuality for its cause, the reason being simply sensuality.

If the clansman gains no wealth while thus working & striving & making effort, he sorrows, grieves, & laments, beats his breast, becomes distraught: 'My work is in vain, my efforts are fruitless!' Now this drawback too in the case of sensuality, this mass of stress visible here & now, has sensuality for its reason....

If the clansman gains wealth while thus working & striving & making effort, he experiences pain & distress in protecting it: 'How will neither kings nor thieves make off with my property, nor fire burn it, nor water sweep it away, nor hateful heirs make off with it?' And as he thus guards and watches over his property, kings or thieves make off with it, or fire burns it, or water sweeps it away, or hateful heirs make off with it. And he sorrows, grieves, & laments, beats his breast, becomes distraught: 'What was mine is no more!' Now this drawback too in the case of sensuality, this mass of stress visible here & now, has sensuality for its reason....

Furthermore, it is with sensuality for the reason, sensuality for the source, sensuality for the cause, the reason being simply sensuality, that kings quarrel with kings, nobles with nobles, brāhmans with brāhmans, householders with householders, mother with child, child with mother, father with child, child with father, brother with brother, sister with sister, brother with sister, sister with brother, friend with friend. And then in their quarrels, brawls, & disputes, they attack one another with fists or with clods or with sticks or with knives, so that they incur death or deadly pain. Now this drawback too in the case of sensuality, this mass of stress visible here & now, has sensuality for its reason....

Furthermore, it is with sensuality for the reason, sensuality for the source...that (men), taking swords & shields and buckling on bows & quivers, charge into battle massed in double array while arrows & spears are flying and swords are flashing; and there they are wounded by arrows & spears, and their heads are cut off by swords, so that they incur death or deadly pain. Now this drawback too in the case of sensuality, this mass of stress visible here & now, has sensuality for its reason....

Furthermore, it is with sensuality for the reason, sensuality for the source...that (men), taking swords & shields and buckling on bows & quivers, charge slippery bastions while arrows & spears are flying and swords are flashing; and there they are splashed with boiling cow dung and crushed under heavy weights, and their heads are cut off by swords, so that they incur death or deadly pain. Now this drawback too in the case of sensuality, this mass of stress visible here & now, has sensuality for its reason, sensuality for its source, sensuality for its cause, the reason being simply sensuality.

MN 13

Sumedhā to her fiancé:

In the face of the Deathless,
what worth are your sensual pleasures?
For all delights in sensuality are
        burning & boiling,
        aggravated, aglow....

A blazing grass firebrand,
        held in the hand:
Those who let go
        do not get burned.

Sensuality is like a firebrand.
        It burns
            those who
            do not let go.

Thig 16:1

Even the more honorable emotions that can develop from sensual attraction—such as love & personal devotion—ultimately lead to suffering & stress when one is inevitably parted from the person one loves.

> Once in this same Sāvatthi there was a certain man whose wife died. Owing to her death he went mad, out of his mind and—wandering from street to street, crossroads to crossroads—would say, 'Have you seen my wife? Have you seen my wife?' From this it may be realized how from a dear one, owing to a dear one, comes sorrow & lamentation, pain, distress, & despair.

> Once in this same Sāvatthi there was a wife who went to her relatives' home. Her relatives, having separated her from her husband, wanted to give her to another against her will. So she said to her husband, 'These relatives of mine, having separated us, want to give me to another against my will,' whereupon he cut her in two and slashed himself open, thinking, 'Dead we will be together.' And from this it may be realized how from a dear one, owing to a dear one, comes sorrow & lamentation, pain, distress, & despair.

> *MN 87*

> How do you construe this, monks: Which is greater, the tears you have shed while transmigrating & wandering this long time—crying & weeping from being joined with what is displeasing, from being separated from what is pleasing— or the water in the four great oceans?...This is the greater: The tears you have shed....Why is that? From an inconstruable beginning, monks, comes transmigration. A beginning point is not evident, though beings hindered by ignorance and fettered by craving are transmigrating & wandering on. Long have you thus experienced stress, experienced pain, experienced loss, swelling the cemeteries—long enough to become disenchanted with all conditioned things, enough to become dispassionate, enough to be released.

> *SN 15:3*

A theme recurrent throughout the Canon is that complete knowledge of any object does not end with an understanding of its allure & drawbacks, but goes on to comprehend what brings emancipation from the mental fetters based on both.

And what is the emancipation from sensuality? Whatever is the subduing of passion & desire, the abandoning of passion & desire for sensuality, that is the emancipation from sensuality.

MN 13

Sundara Samudda:

Ornamented, finely clothed
     garlanded, adorned,
her feet stained red with lac,
     she wore slippers:
          a courtesan.

Stepping out of her slippers—
     her hands raised before me
     palm-to-palm over her heart—
she softly, tenderly,
     in measured words
     spoke to me first:
'You are young, recluse.
     Heed my message:
Partake of human sensuality.
     I will give you luxury.
Truly I vow to you,
     I will tend to you as to a fire.
When we are old,
     both leaning on canes,
then we will both become recluses,
     winning the benefits of both worlds.'

And seeing her before me—
     a courtesan, ornamented, finely clothed,
     hands palm-to-palm over her heart—
     like a snare of death laid out,

apt attention arose in me,
>the drawbacks appeared,
>>disenchantment stood at an even keel:

With that, my heart was released....

>>>>>>>*Thag 7:1*

Seeing a form unmindfully,
>focusing on its pleasing features,
one knows with mind enflamed
>and remains fastened to it.

[Notice how these lines draw directly on the image of burning
as entrapment.]

One's feelings, born of the form,
>grow numerous.
Greed & provocation
>injure one's mind.
Thus amassing stress
>one is said to be far from Unbinding.

[And so on with the rest of the six senses.]

One not enflamed with forms
>—seeing a form with mindfulness firm—
knows with mind unenflamed
>and doesn't remain fastened there.
While one is seeing a form
>—and even experiencing feeling—
it falls away and does not accumulate.
>Faring mindful.
and thus not amassing stress,
>one is said to be
in the presence of Unbinding.

[And so on with the rest of the six senses.]

>>>>>>>*SN 35:95*

There are forms, monks, cognizable via the eye—agreeable, pleasing, charming, endearing, fostering desire, enticing. If a monk relishes them, welcomes them, & remains fastened to them, he is said to be a monk fettered by forms cognizable by the eye. He has gone over to Māra's camp; he has come under Māra's power. The Evil One can do with him as he will.

[And so on with the rest of the six senses.]

SN 35:115

There are forms cognizable by the eye—agreeable...enticing. If a monk relishes them, welcomes them, & remains fastened to them, then...his consciousness is dependent on them, is sustained by them. With sustenance/clinging, the monk is not totally unbound....

If he does not relish them, welcome them, or remain fastened to them, then...his consciousness is not dependent on them, is not sustained by them. Without sustenance/clinging, the monk is totally unbound.

[And so on with the rest of the six senses.]

SN 35:118

Here again, we see the reciprocal nature of attachment: One is bound by what one relishes & latches onto—or rather, by the act of relishing & latching on, in and of itself.

Citta: Venerable sirs, it is just as if a black ox & a white ox were joined with a single collar or yoke. If someone were to say, 'The black ox is the fetter of the white ox, the white ox is the fetter of the black'—speaking this way, would he be speaking rightly?

Some elder monks: No, householder. The black ox is not the fetter of the white ox, nor is the white ox the fetter of the black. The single collar or yoke by which they are joined: That is the fetter there.

Citta: In the same way, the eye is not the fetter of forms, nor are forms the fetter of the eye. Whatever desire & passion arises in dependence on the two of them: That is the fetter there. The ear is not the fetter of sounds....The nose is not the fetter of aromas....The tongue is not the fetter of flavors....The body is not the fetter of tactile sensations.... The intellect is not the fetter of ideas, nor are ideas the fetter of the intellect. Whatever desire & passion arises in dependence on the two of them: That is the fetter there.

SN 41:1

In other words, neither the senses nor their objects are fetters for the mind. Beautiful sights, sounds, & so forth, do not entrap it, nor do the senses themselves. Instead, it is trapped by the act of desire & passion based on such things.

Monks, there are these five strings of sensuality. Which five? Forms cognizable via the eye—agreeable...enticing; sounds... aromas...flavors...tactile sensations cognizable via the body— agreeable...enticing. But these are not sensuality. They are called stings of sensuality in the discipline of the Noble Ones.

The passion for his resolves is a man's sensuality,
not the beautiful sensual pleasures
found in the world.
The passion for his resolves is a man's sensuality.

The beauties remain as they are in the world,
while the wise, in this regard,
subdue their desire.

AN 6:63

Thus sensual pleasures, which belong to the realm of form, are the 'clingable phenomena' that offer sustenance for the bond of desire & passion. Or, to borrow an image from Ven. Rāhula, they are the bait—as long as one is blind to their true nature—for falling into the trap of one's own craving & heedlessness.

Rāhula:

They [the unawakened]:
blinded by sensual pleasures,
          covered by the net,
    veiled with the veil of craving,
          bound by the Kinsman of the Heedless*

          like fish in the mouth of a trap.

Thag 4:8

For this reason, freedom from sensuality as a clinging/suste-
nance requires a two-pronged approach: to realize the true nature
of the bait and to extricate oneself from the trap. The first step
involves examining the unattractive side of the human body, for
as the Buddha says,

> Monks, I don't know of even one other form that stays in a
> man's mind and consumes it like the form of a woman...
> one other sound...smell...taste...touch that stays in a man's
> mind and consumes it like the touch of a woman. The touch
> of a woman stays in a man's mind and consumes it.
>
> I don't know of even one other form that stays in a woman's
> mind and consumes it like the form of a man...one other
> sound...smell...taste...touch that stays in a woman's mind
> and consumes it like the touch of a man. The touch of a man
> stays in a woman's mind and consumes it.

AN 1:1

> Just as if a sack with openings at both ends were full of
> various kinds of grain—wheat, rice, mung beans, kidney
> beans, sesame seeds, husked rice—and a man with good
> eyesight, pouring it out, were to reflect, 'This is wheat. This
> is rice. These are mung beans. These are kidney beans.
> These are sesame seeds. This is husked rice,' in the same
> way, monks, a monk reflects on this very body from the
> soles of the feet on up, from the crown of the head on down,
> surrounded by skin and full of various kinds of unclean
> things:

'In this body there are head hairs, body hairs, nails, teeth, skin, flesh, tendons, bones, bone marrow, kidneys, heart, liver, membranes, spleen, lungs, large intestines, small intestines, gorge, feces, bile, phlegm, pus, blood, sweat, fat, tears, oil, saliva, mucus, fluid in the joints, urine'....

Or again, as if he were to see a corpse cast away in a charnel ground—one day, two days, three days dead—bloated, livid & festering, he applies it to this very body, 'This body, too: Such is its nature, such is its future, such its unavoidable fate'....

Or again, as if he were to see a corpse cast away in a charnel ground, picked at by crows, vultures, & hawks; by dogs, hyenas, & various other creatures...a skeleton smeared with flesh & blood, connected with tendons...a fleshless skeleton smeared with blood, connected with tendons...a skeleton without flesh or blood, connected with tendons...bones detached from their tendons, scattered in all directions— here a hand bone, there a foot bone, here a shin bone, there a thigh bone, here a hip bone, there a back bone, here a rib, there a chest bone, here a shoulder bone, there a neck bone, here a jaw bone, there a tooth, here a skull...the bones whitened, somewhat like the color of shells...piled up, more than a year old...decomposed into a powder, he applies it to this very body, 'This body, too: Such is its nature, such is its future, such its unavoidable fate.' So he abides contemplating the body in & of itself, internally, externally or both internally & externally.

DN 22

The purpose of this contemplation is not to develop a morbid fascination with the grotesque, but simply to correct the distortion of perception that tries to deny the unattractive aspects of the body and to admit only 'the sign of the beautiful'—its attractive side. Now of course this contemplation has its dangers, for it can go overboard into states of aversion & depression, but these are not incurable. At several points in the Canon, where the Buddha sees that monks have let the contemplation of foulness adversely affect their minds, he recommends that they calm their aversion by focusing on the in & out breath as a companion meditation.

Ultimately, as a more balanced perception of the body develops, one may make use of the second prong of the approach: turning one's attention from the object of the lust to the act of lust itself, seeing it as an act of mental fabrication—foolish, inconstant, & stressful—and so removing any sense of identification with it. This, in turn, can calm the mind to an even deeper level and lead on to its Unbinding.

Vaṅgīsa:

With sensual lust I burn.
My mind   is on fire.
Please, Gotama,   out of kindness,
     tell me how to put it out.

Ānanda:

From distorted perception
     your mind is on fire.
Shun the sign   of the beautiful,
                              accompanied by lust.
See fabrications   as other,
                              as stress,
                              not as self.

     Extinguish your great lust.
     Don't keep burning
     again & again.

Thag 21

For one who keeps focusing on the foulness [of the body], any obsession with passion for the property of beauty is abandoned. For one who has mindfulness of breathing well-established to the fore within oneself, annoying external thoughts & inclinations don't exist. For one who keeps focusing on the inconstancy of all fabrications, ignorance is abandoned, clear knowing arises.

Focusing on foulness
    in the body,
mindful
    of in & out breathing,
seeing
    the calming of all fabrications
      —always ardent—
he is a monk who's seen rightly.

    From that he is there set free.

A master of direct knowing,
    at peace,
    he is a sage
gone beyond bonds.

                Iti 85

Sister Nandā:

As I, heedful,
    examined it aptly,
[a vision of a beautiful person
    growing sick, unclean, & putrid]
this body—as it actually is—
    was seen inside & out.

Then was I disenchanted with the body
    and dispassionate within:
Heedful, detached,
    calmed was I,

        unbound.

              Thig 5:4

Views are the second mode of clinging/sustenance. And, as with the abandoning of attachment to sensuality, the abandoning of attachment to views can lead to an experience of Unbinding.

    'I argue for this,'
    doesn't occur to one
    when considering what's grasped
        among doctrines.

Looking for what is   ungrasped
with regard to views,
and detecting inner peace,

I saw.

Sn 4:9

Attachment to views can block an experience of Unbinding in any of three major ways. First, the content of the view itself may not be conducive to the arising of discernment and may even have a pernicious moral effect on one's actions, leading to an unfavorable rebirth.

> I have heard that once the Blessed One was dwelling among the Koliyans....Then Puṇṇa the Koliyan, a bovine, and Seniya, a canine naked ascetic, approached the Blessed One. On arrival, Puṇṇa the Koliyan bovine, bowing down to the Blessed One, sat to one side, while Seniya, the canine naked ascetic, exchanged courteous greetings with the Blessed One, and after an exchange of friendly greetings and courtesies, sat to one side, curling up like a dog. While he was sitting there, Puṇṇa the Koliyan bovine said to the Blessed One, 'Sir, Seniya, this naked ascetic, is a canine, a doer-of-hard-tasks. He eats food that is thrown on the ground. He has long undertaken & conformed to that dog-practice. What is his future destination, what is his future course?'
>
> [The Buddha at first declines to answer, but on being pressed, finally responds:] 'There is the case where a person develops the dog-practice fully & perfectly....Having developed the dog-practice fully & perfectly, having developed a dog's virtue fully & perfectly, having developed a dog's mind fully & perfectly, having developed a dog's demeanor fully & perfectly, then on the break-up of the body, after death, he reappears in the company of dogs. But if he is of such a view as, "By this virtue or practice or asceticism or holy life I will become a greater or lesser god," that is his wrong view. Now, Puṇṇa, there are two destinations for one with wrong view, I say: hell or the animal womb. So the dog-

practice, if perfected, leads him to the company of dogs; if defective, to hell.'

MN 57

Just as if in the last month of the hot season a māluva creeper pod were to burst open, and a māluva creeper seed were to fall at the foot of a sāla tree. The deity living in the tree would become frightened, apprehensive, & anxious. Her friends & companions, relatives & kin—garden deities, forest deities, tree deities, deities living in herbs, grass, & forest monarchs—would gather together to console her: 'Have no fear, have no fear. In all likelihood a peacock is sure to swallow this māluva creeper seed, or a deer will eat it, or a brush fire will burn it up, or woodsmen will pick it up, or termites will carry it off, and anyway it probably isn't really a seed.'

And then no peacock swallowed it, no deer ate it, no brush fire burned it up, no woodsmen picked it up, no termites carried it off, and it really *was* a seed. Watered by a rain-laden cloud, it sprouted in due course and curled its soft, tender, downy tendril around the sāla tree.

The thought occurred to the deity living in the sāla tree: 'Now what future danger did my friends...foresee, that they gathered together to console me?...It's pleasant, the touch of this māluva creeper's soft, tender, downy tendril.'

Then the creeper, having enwrapped the sāla tree, having made a canopy over it, & cascading down around it, caused the massive limbs of the sāla tree to come crashing down. The thought occurred to the deity living in the tree: '*This* was the future danger my friends...foresaw, that they gathered together to console me....It's because of that māluva creeper seed that I'm now experiencing sharp, burning pains.'

In the same way, monks, there are some contemplatives & brāhmans who hold to a doctrine, a view like this: 'There is no harm in sensuality.' Thus they meet with their downfall through sensuality. They consort with women wanderers who wear their hair coiled and long.

The thought occurs to them: 'Now what future danger do
those [other] contemplatives & brāhmans foresee that they
teach the relinquishing & analysis of sensuality? It's
pleasant, the touch of this woman wanderer's soft, tender,
downy arm.'

Thus they meet with their downfall through sensuality.
With the break-up of the body, after death, they will go to a
bad bourn, destitution, the realm of the hungry shades, hell.
There they will experience sharp, burning pains. The
thought will occur to them: '*This* was the future danger
those contemplatives & brāhmans foresaw that they taught
the relinquishing & analysis of sensuality. It's because of
sensuality, as a result of sensuality, that we are now
experiencing these sharp, burning pains.'

MN 45

Secondly, apart from the actual content of the views, a person
attached to views is bound to get into disputes with those who
hold opposing views, resulting in unwholesome mental states for
the winners as well as the losers.

Engaged in disputes in the midst of an assembly,
        —anxious, desiring praise—
    the one defeated is chagrined.
Shaken with criticism, he seeks for an opening.
        he whose doctrine is [judged as] demolished,
        defeated, by those judging the issue:
He laments, he grieves—the inferior exponent—
    'He beat me,' he mourns.

These disputes have arisen among contemplatives.
        In them are elation & dejection.
Seeing this, one should abstain from disputes,
        for they have no other goal
        than the gaining of praise.

He who is praised there
        for expounding his doctrine
        in the midst of the assembly,

laughs on that account & grows haughty,
    attaining his heart's desire.
That haughtiness will be his grounds for vexation,
    for he'll speak in pride & conceit.
Seeing this, one should abstain from disputes.
No purity is attained by them, say the skilled.

                Sn 4:8

Thirdly, and more profoundly, attachment to views implicitly involves attachment to a sense of 'superior' & 'inferior,' and to the criteria used in measuring and making such evaluations. As we saw in Chapter I, any measure or criterion acts as a limitation or bond on the mind.

That, say the skilled, is a binding knot: that
    in dependence on which
    you regard another as inferior.

                Sn 4:5

Whoever construes
    'equal'
    'superior' or
    'inferior,'
by that he'd dispute;
whereas to one unaffected by these three,
    'equal'
    'superior'
do not occur.

Of what would the brāhman* say 'true' or 'false,'
    disputing with whom,
he in whom 'equal,' 'unequal' are not....

As the prickly lotus
is unsmeared by water & mud,
so the sage,
    an exponent of peace,
        without greed,
    is unsmeared by sensuality &
        the world.

An attainer-of-wisdom
isn't measured,
    made proud,
        by views or by what is thought,
        for he isn't affected by them.
He wouldn't be led by action, learning;
doesn't reach a conclusion in any entrenchments.
For one dispassionate toward perception
        there are no ties;
for one released by discernment,
        no delusions.
Those who grasp at perceptions & views
        go about butting their heads in the world.

Sn 4:9

An important point to notice is that attachment to views must be abandoned through knowledge, and not through skepticism, agnosticism, ignorance, or a mindless openness to all views. This point is made clear in the Discourse of the Supreme Net. There the Buddha gives a list of 62 philosophical positions concerning the nature of the self, the cosmos, & the state of ultimate freedom in the immediate present. The list is intended to be exhaustive—the 'net' in the title of the discourse—covering all possible views & positions on these subjects divided into ten categories, one of the categories—equivocation—including cases of agnosticism.

There are, monks, some contemplatives & brāhmans who, being asked questions regarding this or that, resort to verbal contortions, to eel-like wriggling, on four grounds....There is the case of a certain contemplative or brāhman who does not discern as it actually is that 'This is skillful,' or that 'This is unskillful.' The thought occurs to him: 'I don't discern as it actually is that "This is skillful," or that "This is unskillful." If I...were to declare that "This is skillful," or that "This is unskillful," desire, passion, aversion, or irritation would occur to me; that would be a falsehood for me. Whatever would be a falsehood for me would be a distress for me. Whatever would be a distress for me would be an obstacle for me.' So, out of fear of falsehood, a loathing for falsehood, he does not declare that 'This is skillful,' or that 'This is unskillful.'" Being asked questions regarding this or that, he resorts to verbal contortions, to eel-like wriggling: 'I don't think so. I don't think in that way. I don't think otherwise. I don't think not. I don't think not not.'

The second case is virtually identical with the first, substituting 'clinging' for 'falsehood.'

[The third case:] There is the case of a certain contemplative or brāhman who does not discern as it actually is that 'This is skillful,' or that 'This is unskillful'....'If I, not discerning as it actually is that "This is skillful," or that "This is unskillful," were to declare that "This is skillful," or that "This is unskillful"—There are contemplatives & brāhmans who are pundits, subtle, skilled in debate, who prowl about like hair-splitting marksmen, as it were, shooting [philosophical] positions to pieces with their dialectic. They might cross-question me, press me for reasons, rebuke me. I might not be able to stand my ground, that would be a distress for me...an obstacle for me.' So, out of a fear for questioning, a loathing for questioning...he resorts to verbal contortions, to eel-like wriggling....

[The fourth case:] There is the case of a certain contemplative or brāhman who is dull & exceedingly stupid. Out of dullness & exceeding stupidity, he—being asked questions regarding this or that—resorts to verbal contortions, to eel-like wriggling: 'If you ask me if there exists another world [after death], if I thought that there exists another world, would I declare that to you? I don't think so. I don't think in that way. I don't think otherwise. I don't think not. I don't think not not. If you asked me if there isn't another world...both is & isn't...neither is nor isn't...if there are beings who transmigrate...if there aren't...both are & aren't... neither are nor aren't...if the Tathāgata exists after death... doesn't...both...neither...I don't think so. I don't think in that

way. I don't think otherwise. I don't think not. I don't think
not not.'

DN 1

Agnosticism, then, is not a way of abandoning standpoints but
is simply another standpoint: Like all standpoints, it must be
abandoned through knowledge. The type of knowledge called
for—in which standpoints are regarded, not in terms of their content,
but as events in a causal chain—is indicated by the refrain that
follows each of the ten categories of the Supreme Net.

> This, monks, the Tathāgata discerns. And he discerns that
> these standpoints, thus seized, thus grasped at, lead to such
> & such a destination, to such & such a state in the world
> beyond. And he discerns what is higher than this. And yet
> discerning that, he does not grasp at that act of discerning.
> And as he is not grasping at it, bliss [*nibbuti*] is experienced
> right within. Knowing, as they have come to be, the origin,
> ending, allure, & drawbacks of feelings, along with the
> emancipation from feelings, the Tathāgata, monks—
> through lack of sustenance/clinging— is released.

DN 1

Another list of speculative views—a set of ten positions sum-
marizing the standard topics debated by the various schools of
contemplatives in the Buddha's time—recurs frequently in the
Canon. Non-Buddhist debaters used it as a ready-made checklist
for gauging an individual's positions on the controversial issues
of the day and they often put it to the Buddha. Invariably, he
would reply that he did not hold to any of the ten positions.

> 'Seeing what drawback, then, is Master Gotama thus
> entirely dissociated from each of these ten positions?'
>
> 'Vaccha, the position that "the world is eternal" is a thicket
> of views, a wilderness of views, a contortion of views, a
> writhing of views, a fetter of views. It is accompanied by
> suffering, distress, despair, & fever, and it does not lead to

disenchantment, dispassion, stopping; to calm, direct knowledge, self-awakening, Unbinding.

'The position that "the world is not eternal"...
'..."the world is finite"...
'..."the world is infinite"...
'..."the soul is the same thing as the body "...
'..."the soul is one thing and the body another"...
'..."after death a Tathāgata exists"...
'..."after death a Tathāgata does not exist"...
'..."after death a Tathāgata both exists & does not exist"...
'..."after death a Tathāgata neither exists nor does not exist"...does not lead to disenchantment, dispassion, stopping; to calm, direct knowledge, self-awakening, Unbinding.'

'Does Master Gotama have any position at all?'

'A "position," Vaccha, is something that a Tathāgata has done away with. What a Tathāgata sees is this: "Such is form, such its origin, such its disappearance; such is feeling, such its origin, such its disappearance; such is perception... such are fabrications...such is consciousness, such its origin, such its disappearance." Because of this, I say, a Tathāgata— with the ending, fading out, stopping, renunciation & relinquishing of all construings, all excogitations, all I- making & my-making & obsessions with conceit—is, through lack of sustenance/clinging, released.'

MN 72

The construings the Buddha relinquished include views not only in their full-blown form as specific positions, but also in their rudimentary form as the categories & relationships that the mind reads into experience. This is a point he makes in his instructions to Bāhiya, which led immediately to the latter's attaining the goal. When the mind imposes interpretations on its experience, it is engaging implicitly in system-building and all the limitations of location & relationship that system-building involves. Only when it can free itself of those interpretations and the fetters they place on it, can it gain true freedom.

Therefore, Bāhiya, you should train yourself thus: In reference to the seen, there will be only the seen. In reference to
the heard, only the heard. In reference to the sensed, only the
sensed. In reference to the cognized, only the cognized. That
is how you should train yourself. When for you there will be
only the seen in reference to the seen...only the heard...only
the sensed...only the cognized in reference to the cognized,
then, Bāhiya, there is no you in connection with that. When
there is no you in connection with that, there is no you there.
When there is no you there, you are neither here nor yonder
nor between the two. This, just this, is the end of stress.

Ud 1:10

Habits & practices. The Canon mentions a variety of habits &
practices—the third mode of clinging/sustenance. Prominent
among them are Brāhmanical rituals & Jain practices of self-
torture, and according to the Commentary these are the habits &
practices referred to in this context. Yet although the goal will
always remain out of reach as long as one remains attached to
such practices, the abandonment of this attachment is never in &
of itself sufficient for attaining the goal.

But there is another practice which, though a necessary part of
the Buddhist path, can nevertheless offer sustenance for becoming;
and which—as the object of attachment to be transcended—
figures prominently in descriptions of the goal's attainment. That
practice is *jhāna,* or meditative absorption. It might be argued that
this is stretching the term, 'practice' *(vata),* a little far, but jhāna
does not fall under any of the other three sustenances for
becoming at all, and yet it definitely does function as such a
sustenance, so there seems to be little choice but to place it here.

Different passages in the Canon number the levels of jhāna in
different ways. The standard description gives four, although the
pure mindfulness & equanimity attained on the fourth level may
further be applied to four progressively more & more refined formless sensations—termed the 'peaceful emancipations, formlessness
beyond forms'—that altogether give eight levels, often referred to
as the eight attainments.

A number of objects can serve as the basis for jhāna. The breath is one, and an analysis of the Canon's description of the first stages of breath meditation will give an idea of what jhāna involves.

The first step is simply being mindful of the breath in the present:

> There is the case of a monk who, having gone to a forest, to the shade of a tree or to an empty building, sits down folding his legs crosswise, holding his body erect, & keeping mindfulness to the fore. Always mindful, he breathes in; mindful he breathes out.

Then comes evaluation: He begins to discern variations in the breath:

> Breathing in long, he discerns, 'I am breathing in long'; or breathing out long, he discerns, 'I am breathing out long.' Or breathing in short, he discerns, 'I am breathing in short'; or breathing out short, he discerns, 'I am breathing out short.'

The remaining steps are willed, or determined: He 'trains himself,' first by manipulating his sense of conscious awareness, making it sensitive to the body as a whole. (This accounts for the term '*mahaggataṁ*'—enlarged or expanded—used to describe the mind in the state of jhāna.)

> He trains himself, 'I will breathe in sensitive to the entire body'... 'I will breathe out sensitive to the entire body.'

Now that he is aware of the body as a whole, he can begin to manipulate the physical sensations of which he is aware, calming them—i.e., calming the breath—so as to create a sense of rapture & ease.

> He trains himself, 'I will breathe in calming bodily fabrication'... 'I will breathe out calming bodily fabrication.' He trains himself, 'I will breathe in sensitive to rapture'... 'I, will breathe out sensitive to rapture.' He trains himself, 'I

will breathe in sensitive to pleasure'... 'I will breathe out
sensitive to pleasure.'

(As we will see below, he maximizes this sense of rapture &
pleasure, making it suffuse the entire body.)

Now that bodily processes are stilled, mental processes become
apparent as they occur. These too are calmed, leaving—as we will
see below—a radiant awareness of the mind itself.

> He trains himself, 'I will breathe in sensitive to mental
> fabrication'... 'I will breathe out sensitive to mental
> fabrication.' He trains himself, 'I will breathe in calming
> mental fabrication'... 'I will to breathe out calming mental
> fabrication.' He trains himself, 'I will breathe in sensitive to
> the mind'... 'I will to breathe out sensitive to the mind'....
>
> MN 118

The standard description of jhāna, however, does not refer to
any particular object as its basis, but simply divides it into four
levels determined by the way the mind relates to the object as it
becomes more & more absorbed in it.

> Furthermore, monks, the monk—quite secluded from
> sensuality, secluded from unskillful (mental) qualities—
> enters and remains in the first jhāna: rapture & pleasure
> born of seclusion, accompanied by directed thought &
> evaluation. He permeates & pervades, suffuses & fills this
> very body with the rapture & pleasure born of seclusion, so
> that nothing of his entire body is unpervaded by rapture &
> pleasure born from seclusion.
>
> Just as an adept bathman or bathman's apprentice would
> pour bath powder into a brass basin and knead it together,
> sprinkling it again & again with water, so that his ball of
> bath powder—saturated, moisture-laden, permeated within
> & without—would nevertheless not drip; even so, monks,
> the monk permeates...this very body with the rapture &
> pleasure born of seclusion. And as he remains thus

earnest, ardent, & intent, any longings related to the house-hold life are abandoned, and with their abandoning his mind gathers & settles inwardly, unified & composed. That is how a monk develops mindfulness immersed in the body.

And furthermore, with the stilling of directed thoughts & evaluations, he enters & remains in the second jhāna: rapture & pleasure born of concentration, unification of awareness free from directed thought & evaluation—internal assurance. He permeates & pervades, suffuses & fills this very body with the rapture & pleasure born of concentration, so that nothing of his entire body is unpervaded by rapture & pleasure born of concentration.

Just like a lake with spring-water welling up from within, having no inflow from east, west, north, or south, and with the skies periodically supplying abundant showers, so that the cool fount of water welling up from within the lake would permeate & pervade, suffuse & fill it with cool waters, there being no part of the lake unpervaded by the cool waters; even so monks, the monk permeates...this very body with the rapture & pleasure born of concentration. And as he remains thus earnest, ardent & intent...he develops mindfulness immersed in the body.

And furthermore, with the fading of rapture, he remains equanimous, mindful, & alert, and senses pleasure with the body. He enters & remains in the third jhāna, of which the Noble Ones declare, 'Equanimous & mindful, he has a pleasant abiding.' He permeates & pervades, suffuses & fills this very body with the pleasure divested of rapture, so that nothing of his entire body is unpervaded by pleasure divested of rapture.

Just as in a blue-, white-, or red-lotus pond, there may be some of the blue, white, or red lotuses that, born & growing in the water, stay immersed in the water and flourish without standing up out of the water, so that they are per-meated & pervaded, suffused & filled with cool water from their roots to their tips, there being nothing of those blue,

white, or red lotuses unpervaded by cool water; even so,
monks, the monk permeates...this very body with the pleasure
divested of rapture. And as he remains thus earnest, ardent
& intent...he develops mindfulness immersed in the body.

And furthermore, with the abandoning of pleasure & stress—
as with the earlier disappearance of joys & distress—he
enters & remains in the fourth jhāna: purity of equanimity
& mindfulness, neither pleasure nor stress. He sits, permeating the body with a pure, bright awareness, so that nothing
of his entire body is unpervaded by pure, bright awareness.

Just as if a man were sitting covered from head to foot with
a white cloth so that there would be no part of his body to
which the white cloth did not extend; even so, monks, the
monk sits, permeating the body with a pure, bright awareness. And as he remains thus earnest, ardent, & intent...he
develops mindfulness immersed in the body.

MN 119

'Directed thought' mentioned in the reference to the first level
of jhāna corresponds, in the description of breath meditation, to
the mindfulness directed to the breath in the present. 'Evaluation'
corresponds to the discernment of variations in the breath, and to
the manipulation of awareness & the breath so as to create a sense
of rapture & pleasure throughout the body (the bathman kneading
moisture throughout the ball of bath powder). The still waters in
the simile for the third level of jhāna, as opposed to the spring
waters welling up in the second level, correspond to the stilling of
mental fabrications. And the pure, bright awareness in the fourth
level corresponds to the stage of breath meditation where the
meditator is sensitive to the mind.

Thus as the mind progresses through the first four levels of
jhāna, it sheds the various mental activities surrounding its one
object: Directed thought & evaluation are stilled, rapture fades,
and pleasure is abandoned. After reaching a state of pure, bright,
mindful, equanimous awareness in the fourth level of jhāna, the
mind can start shedding its perception (mental label) of the form of
its object, the space around its object, itself, & the lack of activity

within itself. This process takes four steps—the four formless-nesses beyond form—culminating in a state where perception is so refined that it can hardly be called perception at all.

> With the complete transcending of perceptions of form, and the passing away of perceptions of resistance, and not attending to perceptions of diversity, (perceiving,) 'Infinite space,' one enters & remains in the dimension of the infinitude of space....
>
> With the complete transcending of the dimension of the infinitude of space, (perceiving,) 'Infinite consciousness,' one enters & remains in the dimension of the infinitude of consciousness....
>
> With the complete transcending of the dimension of the infinitude of consciousness, (perceiving,)'There is nothing,' one enters & remains in the dimension of nothingness....
>
> With the complete transcending of the dimension of nothingness, one enters & remains in the dimension of neither perception nor non-perception.
>
> *DN 15*

To abandon attachment to jhāna as a sustenance for becoming means, not to stop practicing it, but rather to practice it without becoming engrossed in the sense of pleasure or equanimity it affords, so that one can discern its true nature for what it is.

> When this had been said, Venerable Ānanda asked the Blessed One: 'In the case, lord, where a monk has reached the point that—(perceiving,) "It should not be, it should not occur to me; it will not be, it will not occur to me. What is, what has come to be, that I abandon"—he obtains equanimity. Would this monk be totally unbound, or not?'
>
> 'A certain such monk might, Ānanda, and another might not.'
>
> 'What is the cause, what is the reason, whereby one might and another might not?'

'There is the case, Ānanda, where a monk has reached the
point that—(perceiving,) "It should not be, it should not
occur to me; it will not be, it will not occur to me. What is,
what has come to be, that I abandon"— he obtains
equanimity. He relishes that equanimity, welcomes it,
remains fastened to it. As he does so, his consciousness is
dependent on it, sustained by it. With sustenance, Ānanda,
a monk is not totally unbound.'

'Being sustained, where is that monk sustained?'

'The dimension of neither perception nor non-perception.'

'Then, indeed, being sustained, he is sustained by the
supreme sustenance.'

'Being sustained, Ānanda, he *is* sustained by the supreme
sustenance; for this—the dimension of neither perception
nor non-perception—is the supreme sustenance. There is
[however] the case where a monk...reaches equanimity. He
does not relish that equanimity, does not welcome it, does
not remain fastened to it. Such being the case, his
consciousness is not dependent on it, is not sustained by it.
Without sustenance, Ānanda, a monk is totally unbound.'

MN 106

Once the mind can detach itself from the pleasure & equanimity
offered by jhāna, it can be inclined toward that which transcends
jhāna—the unconditioned quality of deathlessness.

There is the case, Ānanda, where a monk...enters & remains
in the first jhāna: rapture & pleasure born of seclusion,
accompanied by directed thought & evaluation. He regards
whatever phenomena there that are connected with form,
feeling, perception, fabrications, & consciousness as
inconstant, stressful, a disease, a cancer, an arrow, painful,
an affliction, alien, a dissolution, empty, not-self. He turns
his mind away from those phenomena and, having done so,
inclines it to the phenomenon [*dhamma*] of deathlessness:
'This is peace, this is exquisite—the resolution of all

fabrications; the relinquishing of all acquisitions; the ending of craving; dispassion; stopping; Unbinding.'

Staying right there, he reaches the ending of effluents. Or, if not, then—through this very Dhamma-passion, this very Dhamma-delight, and from the total wasting away of the first five Fetters*—he is due to be reborn [in the Pure Abodes], there to be totally unbound, never again to return from that world. [Similarly with the other levels of jhāna.]

MN 64

The fact that the various levels of jhāna are nurtured & willed, and thus dependent on conditions, is important: A realization of exactly how they are nurtured—a realization acquired only through practical experience with them—can give insight into the conditioned nature of all mental events and is one of the ways in which the attachment to jhāna, as sustenance for becoming, can be abandoned.

An indication of how this happens is given in outline form in the Discourse on Mindfulness of In & Out Breathing. To take up the description of breath meditation where we left off: Once there is direct awareness of the mind itself, the various levels of jhāna are reviewed. Now, however, primary attention is focused, not on the object, but on the mind as it relates to the object—the different ways in which it can be satisfied & steadied, and the different factors from which it can be released by taking it through the different levels (e.g., releasing it from directed thought & evaluation by taking it from the first to the second level, and so forth).

He trains himself, 'I will breathe in...& out gladdening the mind.' He trains himself, 'I will breathe in...& out steadying the mind.' He trains himself, 'I will breathe in...& out releasing the mind.'

The states of gladdening, steadiness, & release experienced on these levels, though, are willed and therefore conditioned. The next step is to focus on the fact that these qualities, being conditioned, are inconstant. Once the mind sees directly that inconstancy is inherent both in the pleasure offered by jhāna and in the act of will that brings it about, one becomes dispassionate toward it, stops craving it, and can relinquish any & all attachment to it.

> He trains himself, 'I will breathe in...& out focusing on inconstancy.' He trains himself, 'I will breathe in...& out focusing on dispassion.' He trains himself, 'I will breathe in...& out focusing on stopping.' He trains himself, 'I will breathe in...& out focusing on relinquishing.'
>
> *MN 118*

At the conclusion to the discourse, the Buddha states that breath meditation, when practiced often & repeatedly in this way, results in the maturation of clear knowledge & release.

A more vivid description of how mastery of jhāna can lead to the insight that transcends it, is given in the Discourse on the Analysis of the Properties:

> [On attaining the fourth level of jhāna] there remains only equanimity: pure & bright, pliant, malleable & luminous. Just as if a skilled goldsmith or goldsmith's apprentice were to prepare a furnace, heat up a crucible, and, taking gold with a pair of tongs, place it in the crucible. He would blow on it time & again, sprinkle water on it time & again, examine it time & again, so that the gold would become refined, well-refined, thoroughly refined, flawless, free from dross, pliant, malleable & luminous. Then whatever sort of ornament he had in mind—whether a belt, an earring, a necklace, or a gold chain—it would serve his purpose. In the same way, there remains only equanimity: pure & bright, pliant, malleable & luminous. He [the meditator] discerns that 'If I were to direct equanimity as pure & bright as this toward the dimension of the infinitude of space, I would develop the mind along those lines, and thus this equanimity of mine—thus supported, thus sustained— would last for a long time. [Similarly with the remaining formless states.]'

He discerns that 'If I were to direct equanimity as pure &
bright as this toward the dimension of the infinitude of
space and to develop the mind along those lines, that would
be fabricated. [Similarly with the remaining formless
states.]' He neither fabricates nor mentally fashions for the
sake of becoming or un-becoming. This being the case, he is
not sustained by anything in the world [does not cling to
anything in the world]. Unsustained, he is not agitated.
Unagitated, he is totally unbound right within. He discerns
that 'Birth is ended, the holy life fulfilled, the task done.
There is nothing further for this world.'

MN 140

Doctrines of the self form the fourth mode of clinging/
sustenance. The Canon reports a wide variety of such doctrines
current in the Buddha's time, only to reject them out-of-hand for
two major reasons. The first is that even the least articulated sense
of self or self-identification inevitably leads to stress & suffering.

'Monks, do you see any clinging/sustenance in the form of
a doctrine of self which, in clinging to, there would not arise
sorrow, lamentation, pain, distress, & despair?'

'No, lord.'

'...Neither do I....How do you construe this, monks: If a
person were to gather or burn or do as he likes with the
grass, twigs, branches, & leaves here in Jeta's Grove, would
the thought occur to you, "It's *us* that this person is
gathering, burning, or doing with as he likes"?'

'No, lord. Why is that? Because those things are not our self
and do not pertain to our self.'

'Even so, monks, whatever is not yours: Let go of it. Your
letting go of it will be for your long-term happiness &
benefit. And what is not yours? Form is not yours....

Feeling is not yours....Perception...Fabrications...
Consciousness is not yours. Let go of it. Your letting go of it
will be for your long-term happiness & benefit.'

MN 22

The second reason for rejecting doctrines of the self is that, whatever form they take, they all contain inherent inconsistencies. The
Buddha's most systematic treatment of this point is in the Great
Discourse on Causation, where he classifies all theories of the self
into four major categories: those describing a self (a) possessed of
form & finite; (b) possessed of form & infinite; (c) formless & finite;
and (d) formless & infinite. The text gives no examples for the
categories, but we might cite the following as illustrations: (a)
theories that deny the existence of a soul, and identify the self
with the body; (b) theories that identify the self with all being or
with the universe; (c) theories of discrete souls in individual beings;
(d) theories of a unitary soul or identity immanent in all things.

Discussing these various categories, the Buddha states that
people who adhere to any of them will state that the self already
is of such a nature, that it is destined to acquire such a nature
after death, or that it can be made into such a nature by various
practices. He then goes on to discuss the various ways people
assume a self as defined in relation to feeling.

'In what respect, Ānanda, does one assume when assuming
a self? Assuming feeling to be the self, one assumes that
"Feeling is my self" [or] "Feeling is not my self: My self is
oblivious [to feeling]" [or] "Neither is feeling my self, nor is
my self oblivious to feeling, but rather my self feels, in that
my self is subject to feeling."

'Now, one who says, "Feeling is my self," should be
addressed as follows: "There are these three feelings, my
friend—feelings of pleasure, feelings of pain, & feelings of
neither pleasure nor pain. Which of these three feelings do
you assume to be the self? At a moment when a feeling of
pleasure is sensed, no feeling of pain or of neither pleasure
nor pain is sensed. Only a feeling of pleasure is sensed at that

moment. At a moment when a feeling of pain is sensed, no feeling of pleasure or of neither pleasure nor pain is sensed. Only a feeling of pain is sensed at that moment. At a moment when a feeling of neither pleasure nor pain is sensed, no feeling of pleasure or of pain is sensed. Only a feeling of neither pleasure nor pain is sensed at that moment.

'"Now, a feeling of pleasure is inconstant, compounded, dependent on conditions, subject to passing away, dissolution, fading, & stopping. A feeling of pain...A feeling of neither pleasure nor pain is inconstant...subject to stopping. Having sensed a feeling of pleasure as 'my self,' then with the stopping of one's very own feeling of pleasure, 'my self' has perished. Having sensed a feeling of pain as 'my self'... Having sensed a feeling of neither pleasure nor pain as 'my self,' then with the stopping of one's very own feeling of neither pleasure nor pain, 'my self' has perished."

'Thus he assumes, assuming in the immediate present a self inconstant, entangled in pleasure & pain, subject to arising & passing away, he who says, "Feeling is my self." Thus in this manner, Ānanda, one does not see fit to assume feeling to be the self.

'As for the person who says, "Feeling is not the self: My self is oblivious [to feeling]," he should be addressed as follows: "My friend, where nothing whatsoever is sensed [experienced] at all, would there be the thought, 'I am'?"'

'No, lord.'

'Thus in this manner, Ānanda, one does not see fit to assume that "Feeling is not my self: My self is oblivious [to feeling]."

'As for the person who says, "Neither is feeling my self, nor is my self oblivious to feeling, but rather my self feels, in that my self is subject to feeling," he should be addressed as follows: "My friend, should feelings altogether and every way stop without remainder, then with feeling completely not existing, owing to the stopping of feeling, would there be the thought, 'I am'?"'

'No, lord.'

'Thus in this manner, Ānanda, one does not see fit to assume
that "Neither is feeling my self, nor is my self oblivious to
feeling, but rather my self feels, in that my self is subject to
feeling."

'Now, Ānanda, in as far as a monk does not assume feeling
to be the self, nor the self as oblivious, nor that "My self
feels, in that my self is subject to feeling," then, not assuming in this way, he is not sustained by anything in the world.
Unsustained, he is not agitated. Unagitated, he is totally
unbound right within. He discerns that "Birth is ended, the
holy life fulfilled, the task done. There is nothing further for
this world."

'If anyone were to say with regard to a monk whose mind is
thus released that "The Tathāgata exists after death," is his
view, that would be mistaken; that "The Tathāgata does not
exist after death"...that "The Tathāgata both exists & does
not exist after death"...that "The Tathāgata neither exists nor
does not exist after death" is his view, that would be mistaken.
Why? Having directly known the extent of designation and
the extent of the objects of designation, the extent of expression and the extent of the objects of expression, the extent of
description and the extent of the objects of description, the
extent of discernment and the extent of the objects of discernment, the extent to which the cycle revolves: Having
directly known that, the monk is released. [To say that,]
*"The monk released, having directly known that, does not see,
does not know is his opinion,"* that would be mistaken.' [This
last sentence means that the monk released is not an
agnostic concerning what lies beyond the extent of
designation, and so forth. He *does* know & see what lies
beyond, even though—as Ven. Sāriputta said to Ven.
MahaKotthita—he cannot express it, inasmuch as it lies
beyond objectification. See the discussion on pages 31-32.]

DN 15

Views of the self can center around not only feeling, but also
physical form, perception, fabrications, & consciousness—the five

aggregates for sustenance—which, according to another passage in the above discourse, cover the extent of what can be designated, expressed, & described, but none of which, on investigation, can rightfully be designated as self.

> I have heard that on one occasion the Blessed One was staying at Vārāṇasi, in the Game Refuge at Isipatana. There he addressed the group of five monks:
>
> 'Form, monks, is not-self. If form were the self, this form would not lend itself to dis-ease. One could get form to be like this and not be like that. But precisely because form is not-self, it lends itself to dis-ease. And one cannot get form to be like this and not be like that.
>
> 'Feeling is not-self....Perception is not-self.... Fabrications are not-self....
>
> 'Consciousness is not-self. If consciousness were the self, this consciousness would not lend itself to dis-ease. One could get consciousness to be like this and not be like that. But precisely because consciousness is not-self, it lends itself to dis-ease. And one cannot get consciousness to be like this and not be like that.
>
> 'How do you construe thus, monks—Is form constant or inconstant?'—'Inconstant, lord.'—'And whatever is inconstant: Is it easeful or stressful?'—'Stressful, lord.'—'And is it right to assume with regard to whatever is inconstant, stressful, subject to change, that "This is mine. This is my self. This is what I am"?'—'No, lord.'
>
> '....Is feeling constant or inconstant?...Is perception constant or inconstant?...Are fabrications constant or inconstant?...
>
> 'Is consciousness constant or inconstant?'—'Inconstant, lord.'—'And whatever is inconstant: Is it easeful or stress-ful?'—'Stressful, lord.'—'And is it right to assume with regard to whatever is inconstant, stressful, subject to change, that "This is mine. This is my self. This is what I am"?'—'No, lord.'

'Thus, monks, any form whatsoever that is past, future, or present; internal or external; blatant or subtle; common or sublime; far or near: every form is to be seen as it actually is with right discernment as: "This is not mine. This is not my self. This is not what I am."

'Any feeling whatsoever...Any perception whatsoever...Any fabrications whatsoever...

'Any consciousness whatsoever that is past, future, or present; internal or external; blatant or subtle; common or sublime; far or near: every consciousness is to be seen as it actually is with right discernment as: "This is not mine. This is not my self. This is not what I am."

'Seeing thus, the instructed noble disciple grows disenchanted with form, disenchanted with feeling, disenchanted with perception, disenchanted with fabrications, disenchanted with consciousness. Disenchanted, he grows dispassionate. Through dispassion, he is released. With release, there is the knowledge, "Released." He discerns that "Birth is ended, the holy life fulfilled, the task done. There is nothing further for this world."'

That is what the Blessed One said. Gratified, the group of five monks delighted at his words. And while this explanation was being given, the hearts of the group of five monks, through not clinging [not being sustained], were released from effluents.

SN 22:59

On the surface, doctrines about the self would appear simply to be another variety of speculative view. They deserve separate treatment, though, because they all come down to a deeply rooted sense of 'I am'—a conceit coloring all perception at the most fundamental level.

Monks, any contemplatives or brāhmans who assume in various ways when assuming a self, all assume the five aggregates for sustenance or a certain one of them. Which five? There is the case where an uninstructed, run-of-the-mill person...assumes form to be the self, or the self as possessing form, form as in the self, or the self as in form. He assumes feeling to be the self...perception to be the self... fabrications to be the self...He assumes consciousness to be the self, or the self as possessing consciousness, consciousness as in the self, or the self as in consciousness.

Thus, both this assumption & the understanding, 'I am,' occur to him. And so it is with reference to the understanding 'I am' that there is the appearance of the five faculties—eye, ear, nose, tongue, & body [the senses of vision, hearing, smell, taste, & touch].

Now, there is the intellect, there are ideas [mental qualities], there is the property of ignorance. To an uninstructed, run-of-the-mill person, touched by experience born of the contact of ignorance, there occur [the thoughts]: 'I am,' 'I am thus,' 'I will be,' 'I will not be,' 'I will be possessed of form,' 'I will be formless,' 'I will be percipient [conscious],' 'I will be non-percipient,' or 'I will be neither percipient nor non-percipient.'

The five faculties, monks, continue as they were. And with regard to them the instructed noble disciple abandons ignorance and gives rise to clear knowing. Owing to the fading of ignorance and the arising of clear knowing, [the thoughts]—'I am,' 'I am this,'...'I will be neither percipient nor non-percipient'—do not occur to him.

SN 22:47

The sense of 'I am' can prevent a person from reaching the goal, even when he feels that he has abandoned attachment to sensuality, speculative views, & the experience of jhāna.

There is the case, monks, where a certain contemplative or brāhman, with the relinquishing of speculations about the past and the relinquishing of speculations about the future, from being totally not determined on the fetters of sensuality, and from the surmounting of the rapture of

seclusion [in the first jhāna], of pleasure not-of-the-flesh,
& of the feeling of neither pleasure nor pain [in the fourth
jhāna], thinks, 'I am at peace, I am unbound, I am without
clinging/sustenance!'

With regard to this, the Tathāgata discerns: 'This venerable
contemplative or brāhman, with the relinquishing of
speculations about the past... thinks, "I am at peace, I
am unbound, I am without clinging/sustenance!' Yes,
he affirms a practice conducive to Unbinding. But still
he clings, clinging to a speculation about the past or...
a speculation about the future... or a fetter of sensuality...
or the rapture of seclusion... or pleasure not-of-the-flesh...
or a feeling of neither pleasure nor pain. And the fact that
he thinks, "I am at peace, I am unbound, I am without
clinging/sustenance!"—that in itself points to his clinging.'

With regard to this—fabricated, gross—there is still the
cessation of fabrications. Knowing, 'There is that,' seeing
the escape from it, the Tathāgata has gone beyond it.

MN 102

Whereas the contemplative or brāhman under discussion in
this passage reads an 'I' into what he is experiencing, the Buddha
simply observes that 'There is this....' This unadorned observation—
which simply sees what is present in an experience as present,
and what is absent as absent—is treated in detail in the Lesser
Discourse on Emptiness. There the Buddha describes how to
develop it methodically, in ascending stages passing through the
levels of jhāna—in this case based on the object 'earth', or solidity—
and leading ultimately to Awakening.

Ānanda, just as this palace of Migāra's mother [in the
monastery constructed by Lady Visākhā near Sāvatthi] is
empty of elephants, cattle, & mares, empty of gold & silver,
empty of assemblies of women & men, and there is only
this non-emptiness—the singleness based on the
community of monks; even so, Ānanda, a monk—not
attending to the perception [mental label] of village, not

attending to the perception of human being—attends to the singleness based on the perception of wilderness. His mind takes pleasure, finds satisfaction, settles, & indulges in its perception of wilderness.

He discerns that 'Whatever disturbances that would exist based on the perception of village...that would exist based on the perception of human being, are not present. There is only this modicum of disturbance: the singleness based on the perception of wilderness.' He discerns that 'This mode of perception is empty of the perception of village. This mode of perception is empty of the perception of human being. There is only this non-emptiness: the singleness based on the perception of wilderness.' Thus he regards it as empty of whatever is not there. Whatever remains, he discerns as present: 'There is this.' And so this, his entry into emptiness, accords with actuality, is undistorted in meaning, & pure.

Further, Ānanda, the monk—not attending to the perception of human being, not attending to the perception of wilderness—attends to the singleness based on the perception of earth. His mind takes pleasure, finds satisfaction, settles, & indulges in its perception of earth. Just as a bull's hide is stretched free from wrinkles with a hundred stakes, even so—without attending to all the ridges & hollows, the river ravines, the tracts of stumps & thorns, the craggy irregularities of this earth—he attends to the singleness based on the perception of earth. His mind...settles & indulges in its perception of earth.

He discerns that 'Whatever disturbances that would exist based on the perception of human being...that would exist based on the perception of wilderness, are not present. There is only this modicum of disturbance: the singleness based on the perception of earth.' He discerns that 'This mode of perception is empty of the perception of human being... empty of the perception of forest. There is only this non-emptiness: the singleness based on the perception of earth.' Thus he regards it as empty of whatever is not there. Whatever remains, he discerns as present: 'There is this.'

And so this, his entry into emptiness, accords with actuality, is undistorted in meaning, & pure.

Further, Ānanda, the monk—not attending to the perception of forest, not attending to the perception of earth—attends to the singleness based on the perception of the dimension of the infinitude of space....[and so on through the four levels of formless jhāna. Then:]

Further, Ānanda, the monk—not attending to the perception of the dimension of nothingness, not attending to the perception of the dimension of neither perception nor non-perception—attends to the singleness based on the signless concentration of awareness. His mind takes pleasure, finds satisfaction, settles, & indulges in its signless concentration of awareness.

He discerns that 'Whatever disturbances that would exist based on the perception of the dimension of nothingness... that would exist based on the perception of the dimension of neither perception nor non-perception, are not present. And there is only this modicum of disturbance: that connected with the six sensory spheres, dependent on this very body with life as its condition.' He discerns that 'This mode of perception is empty....[etc.]'

Further, Ānanda, the monk—not attending to the perception of the dimension of nothingness, not attending to the perception of the dimension of neither perception nor non-perception—attends to the singleness based on the signless concentration of awareness. His mind takes pleasure, finds satisfaction, settles, & indulges in its signless concentration of awareness.

He discerns that 'This signless concentration of awareness is fabricated & mentally fashioned.' And he discerns that 'Whatever is fabricated & mentally fashioned is inconstant & subject to stopping.' For him—thus knowing, thus seeing—the mind is released from the effluent of sensuality, the effluent of becoming, the effluent of ignorance. With release, there is the knowledge, 'Released.' He discerns that

'Birth is ended, the holy life fulfilled, the task done. There is nothing further for this world.'

He discerns that 'Whatever disturbances that would exist based on the effluent of sensuality...the effluent of becoming... the effluent of ignorance, are not present. And there is only this modicum of disturbance: that connected with the six sensory spheres, dependent on this very body with life as its condition.' He discerns that 'This mode of perception is empty of the effluent of sensuality...becoming...ignorance. And there is just this non-emptiness: that connected with the six sensory spheres, dependent on this very body with life as its condition.' Thus he regards it as empty of whatever is not there. Whatever remains, he discerns as present: 'There is this.' And so this, his entry into emptiness, accords with actuality, is undistorted in meaning, pure—

superior & unsurpassed.

MN 121

Ānanda: It is said that the world is empty, the world is empty, lord. To what extent is it said that the world is empty?

The Buddha: Insofar as it is empty of self or of anything pertaining to self: Thus it is said that the world is empty. And what is empty of self or of anything pertaining to self? The eye is empty of self or of anything pertaining to self. Forms...Eye-consciousness...Eye-contact is empty of self or of anything pertaining to self.

The ear...The nose...The tongue...The body...

The intellect is empty of self or of anything pertaining to self. Ideas...Intellect-consciousness...Intellect-contact is empty of self or of anything pertaining to self. Thus it is said that the world is empty.

SN 35:85

In abandoning the notion of self with regard to the world—
here defined in the same terms as the 'All' (page 31, above)—the
Buddha did not, however, hold to a theory that there is no self.

> Having sat to one side, Vacchagotta the wanderer said to
> the Blessed One, 'Now then, Venerable Gotama, is there a
> self?' When this was said, the Blessed One was silent.
>
> 'Then is there no self?' Again, the Blessed One was silent.
>
> Then Vacchagotta the wanderer got up from his seat and left.
>
> Then, not long after Vacchagotta the wanderer had left,
> Venerable Ānanda said to the Blessed One, 'Why, lord, did
> the Blessed One not answer when asked a question by
> Vacchagotta the wanderer?'
>
> 'Ānanda, if I, being asked by Vacchagotta the wanderer if
> there is a self, were to answer that there is a self, that would
> be conforming with those contemplatives & brāhmans who
> are exponents of eternalism [i.e., the view that there is an
> eternal soul]. And if I...were to answer that there is no self,
> that would be conforming with those contemplatives &
> brāhmans who are exponents of annihilationism [i.e. that
> death is the annihilation of consciousness]. If I...were to
> answer that there is a self, would that be in keeping with
> the arising of knowledge that all phenomena are not-self?
>
> 'No, lord.'
>
> 'And if I...were to answer that there is no self, the bewil-
> dered Vacchagotta would become even more bewildered:
> "Does the self that I used to have, now not exist?"'
>
> *SN 44:10*

This dialogue is one of the most controversial in the Canon.
Those who hold that the Buddha took a position one way or the
other on the question of whether or not there is a self have to
explain away the Buddha's silence, and usually do so by focusing
on his final statement to Ānanda. If someone else more spiritually
mature than Vacchagotta had asked the question, they say, the
Buddha would have revealed his true position.

This interpretation, though, ignores the fact that of the Buddha's four express reasons for not answering the question, only the last is specific to Vacchagotta. The first two hold true no matter who is asking the question: To say that there is or is not a self would be to fall into one of two philosophical positions that the Buddha frequently attacked as incompatible with his teaching. As for his third reason, the Buddha wanted to be consistent with 'the arising of knowledge that all phenomena are not-self,' not because he felt that this knowledge was worth holding onto in & of itself (*cf.* his statement to Upasiva, on page 28, that in the experience of the goal all phenomena are done away with), but because he saw that the arising of such knowledge could, through causing the mind to let go of all forms of clinging/sustenance, lead to liberation.

This point becomes clear when we compare the exchange with Vacchagotta, given above, to this one with Mogharāja:

> *Mogharāja:*
>
> How does one view the world
> so as not to be seen by Death's king?
>
> *The Buddha:*
>
> View the world, Mogharāja,
>   as empty—
>   always mindful,
> to have removed any view about self.
> This way one is above & beyond death.
> This is how one views the world
> so as not to be seen by Death's king.
>
> *Sn 5:15*

The fundamental difference between this dialogue & the preceding one lies in the questions asked: In the first, Vacchagotta asks the Buddha to take a position on the metaphysical question of whether or not there is a self, and the Buddha remains silent. In the second, Mogharāja asks for a way to view the world so that one can go beyond death, and the Buddha speaks, teaching him to view the world without reference to the notion of self.

This suggests that, instead of being a metaphysical assertion that there is no self, the teaching on not-self is more a strategy, a technique of perception aimed at leading beyond death to Unbinding— a way of perceiving things that involves no self-identification, no sense that 'I am', no attachment to 'I' or 'mine.' And this would be in keeping with the discernment the Buddha recommends in the Discourse on the Supreme Net (see page 64): one that judges views not in terms of their content, but in terms of where they come from and where they lead.

If a person aiming at Unbinding is not to view the world in terms of self, then in what terms should he or she view it? The Buddha's comment to Anurādha (page 25)—'It is only stress that I describe, and the stopping of stress'—suggests an answer, and this answer is borne out by a series of other passages in the Canon.

> 'Lord, "Right view, right view," it is said. To what extent is there right view?'
>
> 'By & large, Kaccāyana, this world is supported by [takes as its object] a polarity, that of existence & non-existence. But when one sees the origination of the world as it has come to be with right discernment, "non-existence" with reference to the world doesn't occur to one. When one sees the stopping of the world as it has come to be with right discernment, "existence" with reference to the world doesn't occur to one.
>
> 'By & large, Kaccāyana, this world is in bondage to attachments, clingings [sustenances], & biases. But one such as this doesn't get involved with or cling to these attachments, clingings, fixations of awareness, biases, or obsessions; nor is he resolved on "my self." He has no uncertainty or doubt that mere stress, when arising, is arising; stress, when passing away, is passing away. In this, his knowledge is independent of others. It's to this extent, Kaccāyana, that there is right view.'
>
> *SN 12:15*

There is the case where an uninstructed, run-of-the-mill person...does not discern what ideas are fit for attention, or what ideas are unfit for attention. This being so, he doesn't attend to ideas fit for attention, and attends [instead] to ideas unfit for attention....This is how he attends inappropriately: 'Was I in the past? Was I not in the past? What was I in the past? How was I in the past? Having been what, what was I in the past? Will I be in the future? Will I not be in the future? What will I be in the future? How will I be in the future? Having been what, what will I be in the future?' Or else he is inwardly perplexed about the immediate present: 'Am I? Am I not? What am I? How am I? Where has this being come from? Where is it bound?'

As this person attends inappropriately in this way, one of six kinds of view arises in him: The view *I have a self* arises in him as true & established, or the view *I have no self*...or the view *It is precisely because of self that I perceive self*...or the view *It is precisely because of self that I perceive not-self*...or the view *It is precisely because of not-self that I perceive self* arises in him as true & established, or else he has a view like this: *This very self of mine—the knower that is sensitive here & there to the ripening of good & bad actions—is the self of mine that is constant, everlasting, eternal, not subject to change, and will endure as long as eternity.* This is called a thicket of views, a wilderness of views, a contortion of views, a writhing of views, a fetter of views. Bound by a fetter of views, the uninstructed run-of-the-mill person is not freed from birth, aging, & death, from sorrow, lamentation, pain, distress, & despair. He is not freed from stress, I say.

The well-taught noble disciple...discerns what ideas are fit for attention, and what ideas are unfit for attention. This being so, he doesn't attend to ideas unfit for attention, and attends (instead) to ideas fit for attention....He attends appropriately, *This is stress...This is the origin of stress...This is the stopping of stress...This is the way leading to the stopping of stress.* As he attends appropriately in this way, three fetters are abandoned in him: identity-view, uncertainty, & grasping at habits & practices.

MN 2

Now this, monks, is the noble truth of stress: Birth is stress, aging is stress, death is stresl; sorrow, lamentation, pain, distress, & despair are stress; association with the unbeloved is stress, separation from the loved is stress, not getting what is wanted is stress. In short, the five aggregates for sustenance are stress.

And this, monks, is the noble truth of the origination of stress: the craving that makes for further becoming— accompanied by passion & delight, relishing now here & now there—i.e., craving for sensual pleasure, craving for becoming, craving for non-becoming.

And this, monks, is the noble truth of the stopping of stress: the remainderless fading & stopping, renunciation, relin- quishment, release, & letting go of that very craving.

And this, monks, is the noble truth of the way leading to the stopping of stress: precisely this noble eightfold path—right view, right resolve, right speech, right action, right livelihood, right effort, right mindfulness, right concentration.

Vision arose, insight arose, discernment arose, knowledge arose, illumination arose within me with regard to things never heard before: 'This is the noble truth of stress'....'This noble truth of stress is to be comprehended'....'This noble truth of stress has been comprehended'....'This is the noble truth of the origination of stress'....'This noble truth of the origination of stress is to be abandoned'....'This noble truth of the origination of stress has been abandoned'....'This is the noble truth of the stopping of stress'....'This noble truth of the stopping of stress is to be realized'....'This noble truth of the stopping of stress has been realized'....'This is the noble truth of the way leading to the stopping of stress'.... 'This noble truth of the way leading to the stopping of stress is to be developed'....'This noble truth of the way leading to the stopping of stress has been developed.'

And, monks, as long as this three-round, twelve- permutation knowledge & vision of mine concerning these four noble truths as they have come to be was not pure, I did not claim to have directly awakened to the unexcelled

right self-awakening....But as soon as this this three-round,
twelve-permutation knowledge & vision of mine
concerning these four noble truths as they have come to be
was truly pure, then did I claim to have directly awakened
to the unexcelled right self-awakening....Knowledge &
vision arose in me: 'Unprovoked is my release. This is the
last birth. There is now no further becoming.'

SN 56:11

Just as if there were a pool of water in a mountain glen—
clear, limpid, & unsullied—where a man with good eyes
standing on the bank could see shells, gravel, & pebbles,
and also shoals of fish swimming about & resting, and it
would occur to him, 'This pool of water is clear, limpid &
unsullied. Here are these shells, gravel & pebbles, and also
these shoals of fish swimming about & resting.' So too, the
monk discerns as it actually is, that 'This is stress....This is
the origination of stress....This is the stopping of stress....
This is the way leading to the stopping of stress....These are
effluents....This is the origination of effluents....This is the
stopping of effluents.... This is the way leading to the
stopping of effluents.' His heart, thus knowing, thus seeing,
is released from the effluent of sensuality, released from the
effluent of becoming, released from the effluent of
ignorance. With release, there is the knowledge, 'Released.'
He discerns that 'Birth is ended, the holy life fulfilled, the
task done. There is nothing further for this world.'

This, great king, is a fruit of the contemplative life, visible
here & now, more excellent than the previous ones and more
sublime. And as for another visible fruit of the contemplative life, higher & more sublime than this, there is none.

DN 2

Thus for the person who aims at Unbinding, the Buddha
recommends a technique of perception that regards things simply
in terms of the four truths concerning stress, with no self-
identification, no sense that 'I am', no attachment to 'I' or 'mine'
involved. Although, as the following passage states, there may be

a temporary, functional identity to one's range of perception, this 'identity' goes no further than that. One recognizes it for what it is: inconstant & conditioned, and thus not worthy of being taken as a self—for in transcending attachment to it, there is the realization of deathlessness.

> Ānanda: 'It is wonderful, lord; it is marvelous. For truly, the Blessed One has pointed out the way to cross over the flood by going from one support to the next. But what then, lord, is the noble liberation?'
>
> The Buddha: 'There is the case, Ānanda, where a noble disciple considers that "Sensual pleasure here & now and in lives to come; form here & now and in lives to come; perceptions of form here & now and in lives to come; perceptions of imperturbability, perceptions of the dimension of nothingness, perceptions of the dimension of neither perception nor non-perception: [All] that is an identity, to the extent that there is identity. [But] this is deathless: the liberation of the mind through lack of clinging/sustenance."'
>
> *MN 106*

Once the sense of self is transcended, its polar opposite—the sense of something standing in contradistinction to a self—is transcended as well. In the Discourse at Kālaka's Park, the Buddha expresses this lack of a self/non-self polarity directly in terms of sensory experience. For a person who has attained the goal, experience occurs with no 'subject' or 'object' superimposed on it, no construing of experience or thing experienced. There is simply the experience in & of itself.

> Monks, whatever in this world—with its gods, Māras & Brahmās, its generations complete with contemplatives & brāhmans, princes & men—is seen, heard, sensed, cognized, attained, sought after, pondered by the intellect: That do I know. Whatever in this world...is seen, heard, sensed, cognized, attained, sought after, pondered by the intellect:

That I directly know. That is known by the Tathāgata, but in the Tathāgata it has not been established ....

Thus, monks, the Tathāgata, when seeing what is to be seen, doesn't construe [an object as] seen, doesn't construe an unseen, doesn't construe [an object] to-be-seen, doesn't construe a seer.

When hearing... When sensing...

When cognizing what is to be cognized, he doesn't construe [an object as] cognized, doesn't construe an uncognized, doesn't construe [an object] to-be-cognized, doesn't construe a cognizer.

Thus, monks, the Tathāgata—being such-like with regard to all phenomena that can be seen, heard, sensed, & cognized— is 'Such.' And I tell you: There is no other 'Such' higher or more sublime.

> Whatever is seen or heard or sensed
>   and fastened onto as true by others,
> One who is Such—among the self-fettered—
> wouldn't further claim to be true or even false.
>
> Having seen well in advance that arrow
>   where generations are fastened & hung
>   —'I know, I see, that's just how it is!'—
> there's nothing of the Tathāgata fastened.

AN 4:24

A view is true or false only when one is judging how accurately it refers to something else. If one is regarding it simply as an event in & of itself, true & false no longer apply. Thus for the Tathāgata—who no longer needs to impose notions of subject or object on experience, and can regard sights, sounds, feelings, & thoughts purely in & of themselves—views are not necessarily true or false, but can simply serve as phenomena to be experienced. With no notion of subject, there is no grounds for 'I know, I see;' with no notion of object, no grounds for 'That's just how it is.' So—although a Tathāgata may continue using 'true' & 'false' in the course of teaching others, and may continue reflecting on right view as a means of abiding mindfully & comfortably in the present—notions of true, false, self, & not self have lost all their holding power over the mind. As a result, the mind can see conditioned events in their suchness—'such are the aggregates, such their origin, such their disappearance'—and is left free to its own Suchness: unrestrained, uninfluenced by anything of any sort.

*   *   *

This concludes our survey of the four modes of clinging/sustenance—passion & delight for sensuality, for views, for habits & practices, and for doctrines of the self—and should be enough to give a sense of *what* is loosed in the Unbinding of the mind. All that remains now is the question of *how*.

Many of the passages we have considered seem to suggest that total Unbinding may be realized by letting go of any one of these four modes of sustenance. What most likely happens in such cases, though, is that the abandoning of one mode immediately triggers an abandoning of the remaining three, for there are other cases reported in the Canon where the experience of Unbinding comes in stages spread over time: the arising of the eye of Dhamma, which frees one from passion & delight for identity views, uncertainty, and grasping at habits & practices; the attainment of Non-returning, which frees one from passion & delight for sensuality; and the attainment of Arahantship, which frees one from passion & delight for all views, the practice of jhāna, & the conceit 'I am.' Why these stages happen in this order, and how they relate to the practices meant to induce them, is what we will take up next.

CHAPTER IV

"And taking a pin, I pulled out the wick."

A THEME recurrent in the passages we have been considering is that the abandonment of clinging/sustenance is effected through knowledge.

> These four [modes of] sustenance have what as their cause, what as their origin, from what are they born, from what do they arise? These four [modes of] sustenance have craving as their cause, craving as their origin, are born from craving, and arise from craving.
>
> And what does craving have as its cause...?...feeling....And what does feeling have as its cause...?...contact....And what does contact have as its cause...?...the six sense spheres.... And what do the six sense spheres have as their cause...?... name & form....And what do name & form have as their cause...?...consciousness....And what does consciousness have as its cause...?...fabrications....And what do fabrications have as their cause...?...ignorance....
>
> And, monks, as soon as ignorance is abandoned in a monk, and clear knowing arises, he—from the fading of ignorance and the arising of clear knowing—clings neither to sensuality as sustenance, nor to views as sustenance, nor to habits & practices as sustenance, nor to doctrines of the self as sustenance. Not clinging [unsustained], he is not agitated. Unagitated, he is totally unbound right within. He discerns that 'Birth is ended, the holy life fulfilled, the task done. There is nothing further for this world.'
>
> *MN 11*

The word *'vijjā'*—translated here as clear knowing—also means 'science.' And just as science implies a method, there is a method—a discipline—underlying the knowledge that leads to Unbinding.

That method is described from a number of perspectives in the Canon, each description stressing different aspects of the steps involved. The standard formula, though, is the noble eightfold path, also known as the middle way.

> There are these two extremes that one who has gone forth is not to indulge in. Which two? That which is devoted to sensuality with reference to sensual objects: base, vulgar, common, ignoble, unprofitable; and that which is devoted to self-affliction: painful, ignoble, unprofitable. Avoiding both of these extremes, the middle way realized by the Tathāgata—producing vision, producing knowledge—leads to calm, to direct knowledge, to self-awakening, to Unbinding.
>
> And what is the middle way realized by the Tathāgata that—producing vision, producing knowledge—leads to calm, to direct knowledge, to self-awakening, to Unbinding? Precisely this noble eightfold path: right view, right resolve, right speech, right action, right livelihood, right effort, right mindfulness, right concentration.
>
> *SN 56:11*

The eight factors of the path fall under three headings, the first two factors coming under discernment, the next three under virtue, and the final three under concentration. These three headings are called the threefold training; the dynamic among them, leading to the knowledge & vision of release, is one of natural cause & effect.

> It is natural that in a virtuous person, one of consummate virtue, freedom from remorse will arise....It is natural that in a person free from remorse gladness will arise...that in a glad person rapture will arise...that for an enraptured person the body will be calmed...that a person of calmed body will feel pleasure...that the mind of a person feeling pleasure will become concentrated...that a person whose mind is concentrated will see things as they have come to be...that a person seeing things as they have come to be will grow

disenchanted...that a disenchanted person will grow
dispassionate...that a dispassionate person will realize the
knowledge & vision of release.

AN 11:2

According to the standard description of the noble eightfold
path, the heading of discernment includes seeing things in terms
of the four noble truths about stress, and maintaining the resolve to
release oneself from sensuality, to abandon ill will, and to avoid
doing harm. Virtue includes abstaining from lying, from divisive
speech, from harsh speech, & from idle chatter; from killing,
stealing, & having illicit sex; and from engaging in dishonest or
abusive forms of making a living, such as dealing in poison, slaves,
weapons, intoxicants, or animal flesh.

The factors that go into concentration, though, are somewhat
more complex.

And what, monks is right effort? There is the case where a
monk generates desire, endeavors, arouses persistence,
upholds & exerts his intent for the sake of the non-arising of
evil, unskillful qualities that have not yet arisen...for the
sake of the abandoning of evil, unskillful qualities that have
arisen...for the sake of the arising of skillful qualities that
have not yet arisen...(and) for the maintenance, non-
confusion, increase, plenitude, development, & culmination
of skillful qualities that have arisen. This, monks, is right
effort.

And what is right mindfulness? There is the case where a
monk remains focused on the body in & of itself—ardent,
alert, & mindful—subduing greed & distress with reference
to the world. He remains focused on feelings in & of
themselves....He remains focused on the mind in & of
itself.... He remains focused on mental qualities in & of
themselves—ardent, alert, & mindful—subduing greed
& distress with reference to the world.

Thus either internally he remains focused on the body in &
of itself, or externally...or both internally & externally...or

else he remains focused on the phenomenon of origination
with reference to the body...or the phenomenon of passing
away with reference to the body...or the phenomenon of
origination & passing away with reference to the body. Or
his mindfulness that 'There is a body,' is maintained just to
the extent of knowledge & recollection. And he remains
independent, not sustained by [clinging to] anything in the
world. [Similarly with feelings, mind & mental qualities.]

DN 22

(See page 66 above, instructions to Bāhiya.)

Right concentration is the practice of the four basic levels of
jhāna.

These three factors are component parts of a single whole. In
fact, their balanced interrelatedness is what makes them 'right.' The
first level of jhāna requires the abandoning of unskillful mental
qualities (the hindrances*), which is part of the duty of right effort;
and, as we saw in the description of breath meditation, jhāna
begins with mindfulness of the present. As jhāna is practiced &
mastered, skillful qualities (such as the factors for Awakening*) are
fostered & maintained; physical processes are stilled so that mental
qualities may become clearly apparent as they occur; mindfulness
is made pure on the attainment of the fourth level of jhāna; and all
four of the establishings of mindfulness are developed.

On whatever occasion, monks, a monk breathing in long
discerns that he is breathing in long; or breathing out long,
discerns that he is breathing out long; or breathing in short
discerns that he is breathing in short; or breathing out short,
discerns that he is breathing out short; trains himself to
breathe in...&...out sensitive to the entire body; trains himself to breathe in...&...out calming bodily fabrication: On
that occasion, monks, the monk remains focused on the
body in & of itself—ardent, alert, & mindful—subduing
greed & distress with reference to the world....

On whatever occasion a monk trains himself to breathe in...
&...out sensitive to rapture; trains himself to breathe in...&...
out sensitive to pleasure; trains himself to breathe in...&...out
sensitive to mental fabrication; trains himself to breathe in...
&...out calming mental fabrication: On that occasion the
monk remains focused on *feelings* in & of themselves—
ardent, alert, & mindful—subduing greed & distress with
reference to the world....

On whatever occasion a monk trains himself to breathe in...
&...out sensitive to the mind; trains himself to breathe in...
&...out gladdening the mind; trains himself to breathe in...
&...out steadying the mind; trains himself to breathe in...&...
out releasing the mind: On that occasion the monk remains
focused on the *mind* in & of itself—ardent, alert, & mindful—
subduing greed & distress with reference to the world....

On whatever occasion a monk trains himself to breathe in...
&...out focusing on inconstancy; trains himself to breathe
in...&...out focusing on dispassion; trains himself to breathe
in...&...out focusing on stopping; trains himself to breathe
in...&...out focusing on relinquishing: On that occasion
the monk remains focused on *mental qualities* in & of
themselves—ardent, alert, & mindful—subduing greed
& distress with reference to the world.

MN 118

In the Great Discourse on the Establishings of Mindfulness, the
Buddha describes mindfulness of mental qualities in & of themselves, in part, in terms of the hindrances and the factors for
Awakening, qualities that are respectively set aside & fostered in
the practice of jhāna.

And how does a monk remain focused on mental qualities
in & of themselves with reference to the five hindrances?
There is the case where, there being sensual desire present
within, a monk discerns, 'There is sensual desire present
within me.' Or, there being no sensual desire present within,
he discerns, 'There is no sensual desire present within

me.' He discerns how there is the arising of unarisen sensual desire. And he discerns how there is the abandoning of sensual desire once it has arisen. And he discerns how there is no further appearance in the future of sensual desire that has been abandoned. [The same formula is repeated for the remaining hindrances: ill will, sloth & torpor, restlessness & anxiety, and uncertainty.]....

And how does a monk remain focused on mental qualities in & of themselves with reference to the seven factors for Awakening? There is the case where, there being mindfulness as a factor for Awakening present within, a monk discerns that 'Mindfulness as a factor for Awakening is present within me.' Or, there being no mindfulness as a factor for Awakening present within, a monk discerns that 'Mindfulness as a factor for Awakening is not present within me.' He discerns how there is the arising of unarisen mindfulness as a factor for Awakening. And he discerns how there is the development & consummation of mindfulness as a factor for Awakening once it has arisen. [The same formula is repeated for the remaining factors for Awakening: investigation of phenomena, persistence, rapture, serenity, concentration & equanimity.]

DN 22

Thus the practice of right mindfulness does not repress undesirable mental qualities—i.e., it does not deny their presence. Rather, it notices them as they occur so that the phenomenon of their occurrence can be understood. Once they are understood for what they are as phenomena, they lose their power and can be abandoned.

However, the practice of right mindfulness focuses, not on the haphazard occurrence of mental qualities, but on the elimination of undesirable qualities—the hindrances—that obstruct jhāna, and on the development of desirable qualities—the factors for Awakening—that jhāna fosters. As these factors are strengthened through the continued practice of jhāna, they make possible a clearer awareness of sensory processes as they occur. The factors of rapture, serenity, & equanimity, existing independently of the input of the five senses, make the mind less involved in sensory pleasures, less inclined to search for emotional satisfaction from them; the factors of mindfulness, investigation of phenomena, persistence, & concentration enable clear insight into the events that make up sensory perception.

To see events in the body & mind simply as that—events, conditioned, arising & passing away—creates a further sense of distance, disenchantment, & de-identification.

> Knowing & seeing the eye as it has come to be, knowing & seeing forms...eye-consciousness...eye-contact as they have come to be, knowing & seeing whatever arises conditioned by eye-contact—experienced as pleasure, pain, or neither pleasure nor pain—as it has come to be, one is uninfatuated with the eye...forms...eye-consciousness...eye-contact... whatever arises conditioned by eye-contact and is experienced as pleasure, pain, or neither pleasure nor pain....
>
> Knowing & seeing the ear....Knowing & seeing the nose.... Knowing & seeing the tongue....Knowing & seeing the body....
>
> Knowing & seeing the intellect as it has come to be, knowing & seeing ideas...intellect-consciousness...intellect-contact as they have come to be, knowing & seeing whatever arises conditioned by mental contact— experienced as pleasure, pain, or neither pleasure nor pain— as it has come to be, one is uninfatuated with the intellect... ideas...intellect-consciousness...intellect-contact...whatever arises conditioned by intellect-contact and is experienced as pleasure, pain, or neither pleasure nor pain.
>
> For him—remaining uninfatuated, unconjoined, unconfused—the five aggregates for sustenance head toward future diminution. The craving that makes for further becoming—accompanied by passion & delight, relishing now this & now that—is abandoned by him. His bodily disturbances & mental disturbances are abandoned. His bodily torments & mental torments are abandoned. His

bodily distresses & mental distresses are abandoned. He is sensitive both to ease of body & ease of awareness.

Any view belonging to one who has come to be like this is his right view. Any resolve, his right resolve. Any effort, his right effort. Any mindfulness, his right mindfulness. Any concentration, his right concentration: just as earlier his actions, speech, & livelihood were already well-purified. Thus for him the noble eightfold path goes to the culmination of its development...the four establishings of mindfulness go to the culmination of their development... the seven factors for Awakening go to the culmination of their development. [And] for him these two qualities occur in tandem: tranquility & insight.

MN 149

With the union of tranquility & insight at the culmination of the path, Awakening occurs. The Canon records many instances where Awakening is sudden & total, and many where it occurs in stages: The reason for the difference isn't stated, but perhaps in sudden Awakening the mind goes through the various stages in quick succession. At any rate, a brief look at the stages will give something of an idea of the dynamics of the mind's Unbinding.

The standard list of the stages gives four, and describes them in terms of how many of the ten Fetters the mind sheds: (1) identity-views, (2) uncertainty, (3) grasping at habits & practices, (4) sensual passion, (5) irritation, (6) passion for form, (7) passion for formlessness, (8) conceit, (9) restlessness, & (10) ignorance.

There are in this community of monks, monks who, with the total ending of [the first] three Fetters, are Stream-winners, steadfast, never again destined for states of woe, headed for self-awakening....

There are...monks who, with the total ending of [the first] three fetters and the waning of passion, aversion, & delusion, are Once-returners. After returning only once to this world they will put an end to stress....

There are...monks who, with the total ending of the first five Fetters, are due to be reborn [in the Pure Abodes], there to be totally unbound, never again to return from that world....

There are...monks who are Arahants, whose effluents are ended, who have reached fulfillment, done the task, laid down the burden, attained the true goal, totally destroyed the fetter of becoming, and who are released through right gnosis.

MN 118

An alternative way of classifying the stages lists three:

There is the case of the monk who has attained full accomplishment with regard to virtue, a modicum of accomplishment with regard to concentration, and a modicum with regard to discernment....

There is the case of the monk who has attained full accomplishment with regard to virtue, full accomplishment with regard to concentration, and a modicum of accomplishment with regard to discernment....

There is the case of the monk who has attained full accomplishment with regard to virtue, full accomplishment with regard to concentration, and full accomplishment with regard to discernment. With the ending of the effluents, he remains in the effluentless release of awareness & release of discernment, having known and made them manifest for himself right in the present.

AN 3:88

As the text makes clear, Stream-winners and Once-returners are those who have fully developed virtue, Non-returners are those who have fully developed virtue & concentration, and Arahants are those who have fully developed all three parts of the path: virtue, concentration, & discernment.

This is not to say, however, that Stream-winners have not developed discernment to a fairly high degree. In fact, the unvarying definition of Stream-winners is that they have 'seen with

discernment,' and their level of Awakening is called the arising of
the Dhamma eye. What they see with this Dhamma eye is always
expressed in the same terms:

> Then Ven. Assaji gave this exposition of Dhamma to
> Sāriputta the wanderer:
>
> > 'Whatever phenomena arise from a cause:
> > > their cause
> > > & their cessation.
> > Such is the teaching of the Tathāgata,
> > > the Great Contemplative.'
>
> Then to Sāriputta the wanderer, as he heard this exposition
> of Dhamma, there arose the dustless, stainless Dhamma
> eye: *Whatever is subject to origination is all subject to cessation.*
>
> *Mv I.23.5*

For this realization to occur, it must follow on a glimpse of what
stands in opposition to 'all that is subject to origination,' i.e., a
glimpse of the Unconditioned—deathlessness.

> [Immediately after winning to the Stream] Sāriputta the
> wanderer went to Moggallāna the wanderer. Moggallāna
> the wanderer saw him coming from afar and, on seeing
> him. said, 'Bright are your faculties, my friend; pure your
> complexion, & clear. Could it be that you have attained the
> Deathless?'
>
> 'Yes, my friend, I have....'
>
> *Mv I.23.5*

Although their Awakening is not yet complete, Stream-winners
see enough of the Deathless to remove all uncertainty about the
Buddha's teachings.

> To Upāli the householder, as he was sitting right there, there
> arose the dustless, stainless Dhamma eye: *Whatever is subject
> to origination is all subject to cessation.* Then—having seen the

Dhamma, having reached the Dhamma, known the Dhamma, gained a footing in the Dhamma, having crossed over & beyond uncertainty, having had no more questioning— Upāli the householder gained fearlessness and became independent of others with regard to the Teacher's message.

MN 56

Their glimpse of deathlessness is also enough to convince Stream-winners of the worthlessness of identity views that center on the five aggregates of sustenance, all of which come under the category of 'all that is subject to origination.'

Māgandiya, it is just as if there were a blind man who couldn't see black objects...white...blue...yellow...red...the sun or the moon. Now suppose that a certain man were to take a grimy, oil-stained rag and fool him, saying, 'Here, my good man, is a white cloth—beautiful, spotless, & clean.' The blind man would take it and wear it.

Then suppose his friends, companions, & relatives took him to a doctor, and the doctor treated him with medicine: purges from above & purges from below, ointments & counter-ointments, and treatments through the nose. And thanks to the medicine his eyesight would appear & grow clear. Then together with the arising of his eyesight, he would abandon whatever passion & delight he felt for that grimy, oil-stained rag. And he would regard that man as an enemy & no friend at all, and think that he deserved to be killed. 'My gosh, how long have I been fooled, cheated, & deceived by that man & his grimy, oil-stained rag!—"Here, my good man, is a white cloth—beautiful, spotless, & clean."'

In the same way, Māgandiya, if I were to teach you the Dhamma—this freedom from Disease, this Unbinding— and you on your part were to understand that freedom from Disease and see that Unbinding, then together with the arising of your eyesight, you would abandon whatever passion & delight you felt with regard for the five aggregates for sustenance. And it would occur to you, 'My gosh, how

long have I been fooled, cheated, & deceived by this mind!
For in clinging, it was just form that I was clinging to...it was
just feeling...just perception...just fabrications... just
consciousness that I was clinging to. With my clinging as
condition, there is becoming....birth...aging & death...sorrow,
lamentation, pains, distresses, & despairs all come into play.
And thus is the origination of this entire mass of stress.'

MN 75

Because they realize that their glimpse of the goal came through
an act of discernment, Stream-winners no longer grasp at habits &
practices. What this means is that they no longer view mere
adherence to habits & practices as a sufficient means to the goal in
& of itself, although they continue to abide by the habits of right
speech, action, & livelihood and by the practice of jhāna that
fostered their discernment to begin with. Having seen the efficacy
of their own actions, they will never intentionally do evil again.
This is what perfects their virtue. Still, they have yet to fully comprehend the practice of jhāna, and so their minds remain attached
to the phenomena—with & without form—on which that practice
is based. As the texts say, they are bound by their incomplete
mastery of concentration & discernment, and by seven remaining
Fetters to the cycle of birth & death.

As for Non-returners, they have mastered jhāna to the extent
that they can use it as a vantage point for watching the arising &
passing away that occurs in reference to the five senses, while the
pleasure, rapture, & equanimity it offers serve them as a fulcrum
point for uprooting any desire for the pleasures of those five senses,
together with all feelings of irritation that come when such desires
are not met.

They, too, have seen the Deathless, but as with Stream-winners,
their discernment is not yet fully comprehensive: They have yet
to turn it on the act of seeing: the tools—tranquility & insight—
that lead to that discernment, and the subtle levels of passion &
delight that accompany it.

The texts express this point in a variety of ways. Some passages
simply list the Fetters that Non-returners have yet to abandon:

passion for form, passion for formlessness, conceit, restlessness, & ignorance. Others give more experiential accounts of what is happening in a Non-returner's mind. From reading these latter accounts it is possible to see how the five Fetters in the list are interconnected: Although Non-returners shed attachment to identity views back when they attained Stream entry, they still have a lingering sense of the conceit 'I am', associated with the five aggregates for sustenance—possessing form & formless—as they function subtly in the arising of tranquility & insight as a process of becoming. And while they have gained enough insight into the five senses to let go of any attachment to them, they still suffer from a certain amount of ignorance concerning the subtler level of becoming inherent in that conceit. This leads to refined forms of passion & delight that keep them restless & bound to the sixth sense: the mind.

> There is the case, Ānanda, where a monk...enters & remains in the first jhāna: rapture & pleasure born of seclusion, accompanied by directed thought & evaluation. He regards whatever phenomena there that are connected with form, feeling, perceptions, fabrications, & consciousness as inconstant, stressful, a disease, a cancer, an arrow, painful, an affliction, alien, a dissolution, empty, not self.
>
> He turns his mind away from those phenomena, and having done so, inclines his mind to the phenomenon [dhamma] of deathlessness: 'This is peace, this is exquisite— the resolution of all fabrications; the relinquishing of all acquisitions; the ending of craving; dispassion; stopping; Unbinding.' Staying right there, he reaches the ending of the effluents. Or, if not, then—through this very Dhamma-passion, this very Dhamma-delight, and from the total ending of the first five Fetters—he is due to be reborn [in the Pure Abodes], there to be totally unbound, never again to return from that world. [Similarly with each of the remaining levels of jhāna.]
>
> *MN 64*

Several strands of our discussion converge at this passage. To begin with, the act of discernment described here—inclining the mind to the Deathless—is identical with the object of concentration described by the Buddha at AN 10:6 (see page 35). This would thus be an instance of tranquility occurring in concert with insight (see page 102).

Secondly, as the passage points out, the crucial difference between Arahants and Non-returners is whether or not the mind feels passion & delight for this act of discernment. Here the distinctions concerning sustenance & clinging raised at the beginning of Chapter III (see page 44) come subtly into play. Any act of discernment, even on this level, comes under the five aggregates for sustenance, as composed of perception, fabrications, & consciousness. If not fully seen for what it is, it can thus act as a phenomenon offering sustenance (or as a clingable phenomenon). Any passion & delight for it—and these themselves are perceptions & fabrications—function as refined sustenance/clinging in the modes of views (of inferior/superior), mental absorption, & a sense of 'I am' involved in the act of discerning. Thus the mind still contains the conditions for becoming on a refined level, and this stands in the way of its total freedom.

> Tied by both
> > the yoke of sensuality
> > & the yoke of becoming,
> beings continue in transmigration,
> > leading to birth & death.

> Those who have abandoned sensuality
> > without reaching the ending of effluents,
> are tied   by the yoke of becoming:
> are said to be   non-returners.

> While those who have cut off uncertainty
> > have no more conceit
> > > or further becoming.

> They who have reached
> > the ending of effluents,

while in the world,
have gone   beyond.

Iti 96

Ven. Khemaka, a Non-returner, speaks shortly before he attains Arahantship: 'Just like the scent of a blue, red, or white lotus: If someone were to call it the scent of a petal or the scent of the color or the scent of a filament, would he be speaking correctly?'

'No, friend.'

'Then how would he describe it if he were describing it correctly?'

'...As the scent of the flower.'

'In the same way, friends, I don't say that this "I am" is form, nor that this "I am" is other than form. I don't say that this "I am" is feeling...perception...fabrications....I don't say that this "I am" is consciousness, nor that this "I am" is other than consciousness. It's just that for me the "I am" with regard to the five aggregates for sustenance has not been removed, although I don't regard them as "This is me."

'...Just like a cloth, spotted & stained, whose owners give it over to a washerman: The washerman scrubs it with salt earth or lye or cow-dung and then rinses it in clear water. Now even though the cloth is clean and spotless, it still has a slight, lingering residual scent of salt earth or lye or cow-dung. The washerman gives it to the owners, the owners put it away in a wicker box filled with incense, and its slight, lingering residual scent of salt earth, lye, or cow-dung disappears.

'In the same way, even though a noble disciple has abandoned the five lower Fetters, he still has with regard to the five aggregates for sustenance a slight, lingering residual "I am" conceit, an "I am" desire, an "I am" obsession. But at a later time he keeps focusing on the phenomena of arising & passing away with regard to the five aggregates of sustenance: "Such is form, such its origination, such its

disappearance. Such is feeling.... Such is perception....Such
are fabrications.... Such is consciousness, such its origination,
such its disappearance." As he keeps focusing on the arising
& passing away of these five aggregates for sustenance, the
slight, lingering residual "I am" conceit, "I am" desire, "I
am" obsession he had with regard to them disappears.'

SN 22:89

Only when discernment is so fully developed & totally comprehensive that it has no lingering conceits, desires, or obsessions for
anything—not even for the fabrications of passion & delight that
condition subtle levels of becoming around the experience of the
deathless—can it complete its emancipation from the six spheres
of sensory contact that make up the All.

Moggallāna [shortly before becoming an Arahant]: Briefly,
lord, to what extent is a monk—released through the
ending of craving—utterly complete, utterly free from
bonds, a follower of the utterly holy life, utterly consummate: foremost among human & heavenly beings?

The Buddha: There is the case, Moggallāna, of the monk
who has heard, *'All things are unworthy of attachment.'*
Having heard that all things are unworthy of attachment,
he fully knows every thing. Fully knowing every thing,
he fully comprehends every thing. Fully comprehending
every thing, then whatever feeling he experiences—
pleasure, pain, neither pleasure nor pain— he keeps
focusing on inconstancy with regard to it, keeps focusing
on dispassion, focusing on stopping, focusing on
relinquishing. As he keeps focusing on inconstancy...
dispassion...stopping...relinquishing with regard to that
feeling, he is unsustained by [does not cling to] anything
in the world. Unsustained, he is not agitated. Unagitated,
he is unbound right within. He discerns: 'Birth is ended,
the holy life fulfilled, the task done. There is nothing
further for this world.'

It's to this extent, Moggallāna, that a monk, in brief, is
released through the ending of craving, utterly complete,

utterly free from bonds, a follower of the utterly holy life, utterly consummate: foremost among human & heavenly beings.

AN 7:58

Knowing the All
    from all around,
not passionate
    for any aims at all:
He, having comprehended
    the All,
has gone beyond
    all stress.

Iti 7

Now when a monk discerns—as they actually are—the origin & passing away of the six spheres of (sensory) contact, their allure, their drawbacks, & the emancipation from them, then he discerns what is superior to all these things.

DN 1

With ignorance as condition, there occur fabrications; with fabrications as condition, [sensory] consciousness; with [sensory] consciousness as condition, name & form; with name & form as condition, the six sense spheres....

But with the remainderless fading & stopping of ignorance, fabrications stop. With the stopping of fabrications, [sensory] consciousness stops. With the stopping of [sensory] consciousness, name & form...the six sense spheres...contact... feeling...craving...clinging...becoming... birth stops. With the stopping of birth, then aging & death, sorrow, lamentation, pain, & distress all stop. Thus is the stopping of this entire mass of stress.

MN 115

That which arises in dependence on the eye as pleasure or joy, that is the allure of the eye. Whatever [aspects] of the eye are inconstant, stressful, & subject to change, that is the drawback of the eye. Whatever is the subduing of passion & desire, the abandoning of passion & desire for the eye, that

is the emancipation from the eye. [Similarly with the ear,
nose, tongue, body, & intellect, and with forms, sounds,
aromas, flavors, tactile sensations, & ideas.]

SN 35:13-14

This, the unsurpassed, foremost state of peace, has been
realized by the Tathāgata: liberation, through lack of
clinging/sustenance, having known, as they actually are,
the origin, the passing away, the allure, the drawbacks of—
and the emancipation from—the six spheres of (sensory)
contact.

MN 102

This unsurpassed, foremost state of peace that comes as the
mind realizes emancipation from the All, is totally Unconditioned.

There is, monks, an unborn—unbecome—unmade—
uncompounded. If there were not that unborn—unbecome—
unmade—uncompounded, there would not be the case that
emancipation from the born—become—made—compounded
would be discerned. But precisely because there is an
unborn—unbecome—unmade—uncompounded, emancipation from the born—become—made—compounded is
thus discerned.

Ud 8:3

Where water, earth, fire and wind have no footing:
There the stars do not shine,
    the sun is not visible,,
    the moon does not appear,
    darkness is not found.

And when a brāhman, a sage through sagacity,
    has known [this] for himself,
then from form & formless,
    from pleasure & pain,

      he is freed.

Ud 2:10

Having fully realized the Unconditioned, the mind no longer falls under the sway of stress & inconstancy. No longer engrossed, it finds that its sense of participation & engagement in all the processes of experience disbands once & for all.

> Nandaka: 'Sisters, it is just as if an adept butcher or butcher's apprentice, having killed a cow, were to carve it up with a sharp carving knife so that—without damaging the substance of the inner flesh, without damaging the substance of the outer hide—he would cut, sever, & detach only the skin muscles, connective tissues, & attachments in between; and having cut, severed, & detached the outer skin, and then covering the cow again with that very skin, he were to say that the cow was actually joined to the skin: Would he be speaking rightly?'
>
> 'No, sir. Why is that?...because no matter how much he might say that the cow was actually joined to the skin, the cow would still be disjoined from the skin.'
>
> 'This simile, sisters, I have given to convey a message. The message is this: The substance of the inner flesh stands for the six inner sense spheres [the senses]; the substance of the outer hide stands for the six outer sense spheres [their objects]. The skin muscles, connective tissues, & attachments in between stand for passion & delight. And the sharp knife stands for noble discernment, which cuts, severs, & detaches the defilements, fetters, & attachments in between.'
>
> *MN 146*

Although the senses & their objects are there just as before, the fundamental affective link that ties the mind to sensations has been cut. And its cutting means unconditional freedom for the mind.

> MahāKaccāyana: 'Concerning the brief statement the Blessed One made, after which he entered his dwelling without expounding the detailed meaning—i.e., "A monk should investigate in such a way that, his consciousness neither externally scattered & diffused, nor internally

fixated, he would from lack of clinging/sustenance be unagitated. When...from lack of clinging/sustenance he would be unagitated, there is no seed for the conditions of future birth, aging, death, or stress"—I understand the detailed meaning of this statement to be this:

'How is consciousness said to be scattered & diffused? There is the case where a form is seen with the eye, and consciousness follows the drift of [lit.: 'flows after'] the image of the form, is tied to the attraction of the image of the form, is chained to the attraction of the image of the form, is fettered & joined to the attraction of the image of the form: Consciousness is said to be externally scattered & diffused. [Similarly with the remaining senses.]

'And how is consciousness said not to be externally scattered & diffused? There is the case where a form is seen with the eye, and consciousness does not follow the drift of the image of the form, is not tied to...chained to...fettered, or joined to the attraction of the image of the form: Consciousness is said not to be externally scattered & diffused. [Similarly with the remaining senses.]

'And how is the mind said to be internally fixated? There is the case where a monk...enters & remains in the first jhāna. His consciousness follows the drift of the rapture & pleasure born of seclusion, is tied to...chained...fettered, & joined to the attraction of the rapture & pleasure born of seclusion. Or further...he enters & remains in the second jhāna. His consciousness follows the drift of the rapture & pleasure born of concentration, is tied to...chained...fettered, & joined to the attraction of the rapture & pleasure born of concentration. Or further...he enters & remains in the third jhāna....His consciousness follows the drift of the equanimity & pleasure....Or further...he enters & remains in the fourth jhāna. His consciousness follows the drift of the neither pleasure nor pain, is tied to...chained to...fettered, & joined to the attraction of the neither pleasure nor pain: The mind is said to be internally fixated.

'And how is the mind said not to be internally fixated? There is the case where a monk...enters & remains in the first jhāna. His consciousness does not follow the drift of the rapture & pleasure born of seclusion, is not tied to...chained to...fettered, or joined to the rapture & pleasure born of seclusion. [Similarly with the remaining levels of jhāna.]

'And how is agitation caused by clinging/sustenance? There is the case of an uninstructed, run-of-the-mill person...who assumes form to be the self, or the self as possessing form, or form as in the self, or the self as in form. His form changes & is unstable. Because of the change & instability of his form, consciousness alters in accordance with the change in the form. With the concomitant arising of agitation born from this alteration, the mind stays consumed. And because of the consumption of awareness, he feels fearful, threatened, & solicitous. It is thus, friends, that agitation is caused by clinging/sustenance. [Similarly with feeling, perception, fabrications, & consciousness.]

'And how is non-agitation caused by lack of clinging/ sustenance? There is the case of an instructed noble disciple...who does not assume form to be the self, or the self as possessing form, or t form as in the self, or the self as in form. His form changes & is unstable, but consciousness does not for that reason alter in accordance with the change in t form. His mind is not consumed with any concomitant agitation born from such a change. Because his awareness is not consumed, he does not feel fearful, threatened, or solicitous. It is thus, friends, that non-agitation is caused by lack of clinging/sustenance. [Similarly with feeling, perception, fabrications & consciousness.]'

MN 138

One who is dependent has wavering. One who is independent has no wavering. There being no wavering, there is calm. There being calm, there is no desire. There being no desire, there is no coming or going. There being no coming or going, there is no passing away or arising. There being no

passing away or arising, there is neither a here nor a there
nor a between-the-two. This, just this, is the end of stress.

Ud 8:4

Sensing a feeling of pleasure, he [a person who has reached
the goal: This is the continuation of the passage on pages
74-75] discerns that it is fleeting, not grasped at, not relished.
Sensing a feeling of pain....Sensing a feeling of neither
pleasure nor pain, he discerns that it is fleeting, not grasped
at, not relished. Sensing a feeling of pleasure, he senses it
disjoined from it. Sensing a feeling of pain....Sensing a
feeling of neither pleasure nor pain, he senses it disjoined
from it. When sensing a feeling limited to the body, he
discerns that 'I am sensing a feeling limited to the body.'
When sensing a feeling limited to life, he discerns that 'I am
sensing a feeling limited to life.' He discerns that 'With the
break-up of the body, after the termination of life, all that is
experienced, not being relished, will grow cold right here.'

Just as an oil lamp burns in dependence on oil & wick; and
from the termination of the oil & wick—and from not being
provided any other sustenance—it goes out unnourished;
even so, when sensing a feeling limited to the body, he
discerns that 'I am sensing a feeling limited to the body.'
When sensing a feeling limited to life, he discerns that 'I am
sensing a feeling limited to life.' He discerns that 'With the
break-up of the body, after the termination of life, all that is
sensed, not being relished, will grow cold right here.'

Thus a monk so endowed is endowed with the highest
resolve for discernment, for this—the knowledge of the
ending of all stress—is the highest noble discernment.

His release, being founded on truth, does not fluctuate, for
whatever is deceptive is false; Unbinding—the undeceptive—
is true. Thus a monk so endowed is endowed with the highest resolve for truth, for this—Unbinding, the undeceptive—
is the highest noble truth.

Whereas formerly he foolishly had taken on & brought to
completion (mental) acquisitions, he has now abandoned

them, their root destroyed, made like a palmyra stump,
deprived of the conditions of development, not destined
for future arising. Thus a monk so endowed is endowed
with the highest resolve for relinquishing, for this—the
renunciation of all acquisitions—is the highest noble
relinquishing.

Whereas formerly he foolishly had greed—as well as desire
& infatuation—he has now abandoned them, their root
destroyed...not destined for future arising. Whereas
formerly he foolishly had malice—as well as ill-will &
hatred—he has now abandoned them....Whereas formerly
he foolishly had ignorance—as well as delusion &
confusion—he has now abandoned them, their root
destroyed, made like a palmyra stump, deprived of the
conditions of development, not destined for future arising.
Thus a monk so endowed is endowed with the highest
resolve for calm, for this—the calming of passions,
aversions, & delusions—is the highest noble calm. 'One
should not be negligent of discernment, should guard the
truth, be devoted to relinquishing, and train only for calm.'
Thus it was said, and in reference to this was it said.

'He has been stilled where the currents of construing do not
flow. And when the currents of construing do not flow, he
is said to be a sage at peace:' Thus it has been said. With
reference to what was it said? 'I am' is a construing. 'I am
this' is a construing. 'I will be' is a construing. 'I will not
be'...'I will be possessed of form'...'I will not be possessed
of form'...'I will be percipient'...'I will not be percipient'...
'I will be neither percipient nor non-percipient' is a construing. Construing is a disease, construing is a cancer,
construing is an arrow. By going beyond all construing,
he is called a sage at peace.

Furthermore, a sage at peace isn't born, doesn't age, doesn't
die, is unagitated and free from longing. He doesn't have
anything whereby he would be born. Not being born, will he
age? Not aging, will he die? Not dying, will he be agitated?
Not being agitated, for what will he long? It was in reference

to this that it was said, 'He has been stilled where the currents of construing do not flow. And when the currents of construing do not flow, he is said to be a sage at peace.'

MN 140

Sāriputta: And how, my friend, is a monk's mind well-composed by means of awareness? 'My mind is without passion'—his mind is well-composed by means of awareness. 'My mind is without aversion'....'My mind is without delusion'....'My mind is not subject to passion'...'to aversion'...'to delusion'—his mind is well-composed by means of awareness. 'My mind is destined not to return to states of sensuality'...'to states of form'...'to formless states'— his mind is well-composed by means of awareness.

Even if powerful forms cognizable by the eye come into the visual range of a monk whose mind is thus rightly released, his mind is neither overpowered nor even engaged. Being still, having reached imperturbability, he focuses on their passing away. And even if powerful sounds...aromas...flavors...tactile sensations....Even if powerful ideas cognizable by the intellect come into the mental range of a monk whose mind is thus rightly released, his mind is neither overpowered nor even engaged. Being still, having reached imperturbability, he focuses on their passing away.

Just as if there were a stone column, sixteen spans tall, of which eight spans were rooted below ground, and then from the east there were to come a powerful wind storm: The column would not shiver nor quiver nor quake. And then from the west...the north...the south there were to some a powerful wind storm: The column would not shiver nor quiver nor quake. Why? Because of the depth of

the root and the well-buriedness of the stone column. In the same way, my friend, even if powerful forms cognizable by the eye come into the visual range of a monk whose mind is thus rightly released...etc....his mind is neither overpowered nor even engaged.

AN 9:26

Everywhere
    the sage
        independent
holds nothing dear or undear.

    In him
lamentation & selfishness
like water on a white lotus
    do not adhere.

As a water bead on a lotus leaf,
as water on a red lily,
    doesn't adhere,

    so the sage
    doesn't adhere
    in connection
with the seen, the heard, or the sensed;

    for, cleansed,
    he doesn't construe
by means of the seen, the heard, or the sensed.

    In no other way
does he wish for purity,
for he neither takes on passion
    nor puts it away.

Sn 4:6

This radical freedom—unattached to sensation, untouched by the power of passion, aversion, & delusion—is the Unbinding experienced in the present life.

Sister Pāṭācārā:

Washing my feet, I noticed
    the
    water.

And in watching it flow from high
    to
    low,

my heart was composed
like a fine thoroughbred steed.

Then taking a lamp, I entered the hut,
checked the bedding,
sat down on the bed.

And taking a pin, I pulled out the wick:
Like the flame's unbinding
was the liberation
of awareness.

Thig 5:10

End Notes

Becoming *(bhava):* States of sensuality, form, & formlessness that can develop from craving & clinging, and provide the condition for birth on both the internal & external levels.

Binding *(vāna):* Related terms *(cf. nibbāna—nibbuta)* would be *vivaṭa,* open; *sanvuta,* closed, restrained, tied up; & *parivuta,* surrounded. See PTS Dictionary, *Varati and *Vuṇāti.

Brāhman: The brāhmans of India have long maintained that they, by their birth, are worthy of the highest respect. Buddhists borrowed the term, 'brāhman,' to apply to those who have attained the goal, to show that respect is earned not by birth, race, or caste, but by spiritual attainment.

Effluent *(āsava):* Four qualities—sensuality, views, becoming, & ignorance—that 'flow out' of the mind and create the flood *(ogha)* of the round of death & rebirth.

Factors for Awakening *(sambojjhaṅga):* The seven qualities, developed through jhāna, that lead the mind to Awakening are (1) mindfulness, (2) analysis of phenomena, (3) persistence, (4) rapture, (5) serenity, (6) concentration, & (7) equanimity.

Fetters *(sanyojana):* The ten Fetters that bind the mind to the round of death & rebirth are (1) identity views, (2) uncertainty, (3) grasping at habits & practices, (4) sensual passion, (5) irritation, (6) passion for form, (7) passion for formlessness, (8) conceit, (9) restlessness, & (10) ignorance.

Hindrances *(nīvaraṇa):* The five hindrances that prevent the mind from gaining concentration are (1) sensual desire, (2) ill will, (3) sloth & torpor, (4) restlessness & anxiety, and (5) uncertainty.

Kinsman of the Heedless: An epithet for Māra.

Māra: The personification of evil & temptation.

Nāga: A term commonly used to refer to strong, stately, & heroic animals, such as elephants & magical serpents. In Buddhism, it is also used to refer to those who have attained the goal.

Stress *(dukkha):* *Dukkha,* which is traditionally translated in the Commentaries as, 'that which is hard to bear,' is notorious for having no truly adequate equivalent in English, but 'stress'—in its basic sense as a strain on body or mind—seems to be as close as English can get. In the Pali Canon, dukkha applies both to physical & to mental phenomena, ranging from the intense stress of acute anguish or pain to the innate burdensomeness of even the most subtle mental or physical fabrications.

Such *(tādī):* An adjective to describe one who has attained the goal. It indicates that the person's state is indefinable but not subject to change or influences of any sort.

Tathāgata: Literally, 'one who has become real *(tatha-āgata)'* or 'one who has truly gone *(tathā-gata),'* an epithet used in ancient India for a person who has attained the highest religious goal. In Buddhism, it usually refers specifically to the Buddha, although occasionally it also refers to any of his disciples who have attained the Buddhist goal.

Bibliography

Blair, Chauncey J. *Heat in the Rig Veda and Atharva Veda*. (New Haven: American Oriental Society, 1961.)

Buddhaghosa, Bhadantācariya. *The Path of Purification*, trans. by Bhikkhu Ñāṇamoli. (Kandy: Buddhist Publication Society, 1975.)

Collins, Steven. *Selfless Persons: Imagery and Thought in Theravāda Buddhism*. (Cambridge: Cambridge University Press, 1982.)

Ergardt, Jan T. *Faith and Knowledge in Early Buddhism*. (Leiden: E. J. Brill, 1977.)

Gonda, Jan. *Some Observations on the Relations between 'Gods' and 'Powers' in the Veda, a propos of the Phrase, sunuh sahasah*. (s'Gravenhage: Mouton & Co., 1957.)

Griffith, Ralph (trans.). *The Hymns of the Rig Veda*. (Varanasi: The Chowkhamba Sanskrit Series Office, 1963.)

Jayatilleke, K. N. *Early Buddhist Theory of Knowledge*. (London: George Allen & Unwin Ltd., 1963.)

Johansson, Rune E. A. *The Psychology of Nirvāṇa*. (London: George Allen & Unwin Ltd., 1969.)

Knipe, David M. *In the Image of Fire: The Vedic Experiences of Heat*. (Delhi: Motilal Banarsidass, 1975.)

Ñāṇananda, Bhikkhu. *Concept and Reality in Early Buddhist Thought*. (Kandy: Buddhist Publication Society, 1971.)

_____. *The Magic of the Mind: An Exposition of the Kalakarama Sutta*. (Kandy: Buddhist Publication Society, 1974.)

Nyanaponika Thera. *Anattā and Nibbāna: Egolessness and Deliverance*. (Kandy: Buddhist Publication Society, 1971.)

O'Flaherty, Wendy Doniger. *The Rig Veda: An Anthology*. (Harmondsworth: Penguin Books Ltd., 1984.)

Pali Text Society's *Pali-English Dictionary.* Ed. T. W. Rhys Davids and W. Stede. (London: Routledge & Kegan Paul Ltd., 1972.)

Panikkar, Raimundo. *The Vedic Experience.* (Berkeley: University of California Press, 1977.)

Radhakrishnan, S. (ed. & trans.). *The Principal Upaniṣads.* (London: George Allen & Unwin, 1953.)

Warder, A. K. *Outline of Indian Philosophy.* (Delhi: Motilal Banarsidass, 1971.)

Index